D1400383

Poverty

Other Books of Related Interest:

At Issue Series
Are Executives Paid Too Much?
How Can the Poor Be Helped?

Current Controveries Series
Developing Nations

Global Viewpoints Series
Human Rights

Issues That Concern You Series
Consumer Culture

Opposing Viewpoints Series
Population
Unemployment
Welfare

GLOBALVIEWPOINTS

Poverty

Noël Merino, Book Editor

GREENHAVEN PRESS
A part of Gale, Cengage Learning

Property of
Baker College
of Allen Park

GALE
CENGAGE Learning·

Detroit • New York • San Francisco • New Haven, Conn • Waterville, Maine • London

Elizabeth Des Chenes, *Managing Editor*

© 2012 Greenhaven Press, a part of Gale, Cengage Learning

Gale and Greenhaven Press are registered trademarks used herein under license.

For more information, contact:
Greenhaven Press
27500 Drake Rd.
Farmington Hills, MI 48331-3535
Or you can visit our Internet site at gale.cengage.com

For product information and technology assistance, contact us at

Gale Customer Support, 1-800-877-4253
For permission to use material from this text or product, submit all requests online at www.cengage.com/permissions

Further permissions questions can be emailed to permissionrequest@cengage.com

Articles in Greenhaven Press anthologies are often edited for length to meet page requirements. In addition, original titles of these works are changed to clearly present the main thesis and to explicitly indicate the author's opinion. Every effort is made to ensure that Greenhaven Press accurately reflects the original intent of the authors. Every effort has been made to trace the owners of copyrighted material.

Cover image copyright © Trevor Kittelty/Shutterstock.com.

LIBRARY OF CONGRESS CATALOGING-IN-PUBLICATION DATA

Poverty / Noël Merino, book editor.
    p. cm. -- (Global viewpoints)
    Includes bibliographical references and index.
    ISBN 978-0-7377-5662-3 (hbk.) -- ISBN 978-0-7377-5663-0 (pbk.)
    1. Poverty. I. Merino, Noël.
    HC79.P6P678 2012
    339.4'6--dc23
                                                                    2011046483

Printed in Mexico
1 2 3 4 5 6 7 16 15 14 13 12

Contents

Chapter 2: The Experience of Poverty Around the World

Chapter 3: The Causes of Poverty

Chapter 4: Efforts to End Poverty

Poverty can only be eliminated by trade-fueled growth that allows private businesses to prosper, but current practices are undermining fair trade.

Foreword

> "The problems of all of humanity can
> only be solved by all of humanity."
>   —Swiss author Friedrich Dürrenmatt

Global interdependence has become an undeniable reality. Mass media and technology have increased worldwide access to information and created a society of global citizens. Understanding and navigating this global community is a challenge, requiring a high degree of information literacy and a new level of learning sophistication.

Building on the success of its flagship series, Opposing Viewpoints, Greenhaven Press has created the Global Viewpoints series to examine a broad range of current, often controversial topics of worldwide importance from a variety of international perspectives. Providing students and other readers with the information they need to explore global connections and think critically about worldwide implications, each Global Viewpoints volume offers a panoramic view of a topic of widespread significance.

Drugs, famine, immigration—a broad, international treatment is essential to do justice to social, environmental, health, and political issues such as these. Junior high, high school, and early college students, as well as general readers, can all use Global Viewpoints anthologies to discern the complexities relating to each issue. Readers will be able to examine unique national perspectives while, at the same time, appreciating the interconnectedness that global priorities bring to all nations and cultures.

Material in each volume is selected from a diverse range of sources, including journals, magazines, newspapers, nonfiction books, speeches, government documents, pamphlets, organization newsletters, and position papers. Global Viewpoints is truly global, with material drawn primarily from international sources available in English and secondarily from US sources with extensive international coverage.

Features of each volume in the Global Viewpoints series include:

- An **annotated table of contents** that provides a brief summary of each essay in the volume, including the name of the country or area covered in the essay.

- An **introduction** specific to the volume topic.

- A **world map** to help readers locate the countries or areas covered in the essays.

- For each viewpoint, an **introduction** that contains notes about the author and source of the viewpoint explains why material from the specific country is being presented, summarizes the main points of the viewpoint, and offers three **guided reading questions** to aid in understanding and comprehension.

- **For further discussion** questions that promote critical thinking by asking the reader to compare and contrast aspects of the viewpoints or draw conclusions about perspectives and arguments.

- A worldwide list of **organizations to contact** for readers seeking additional information.

- A **periodical bibliography** for each chapter and a **bibliography of books** on the volume topic to aid in further research.

- A comprehensive **subject index** to offer access to people, places, events, and subjects cited in the text, with the countries covered in the viewpoints highlighted.

Global Viewpoints is designed for a broad spectrum of readers who want to learn more about current events, history, political science, government, international relations, economics, environmental science, world cultures, and sociology—students doing research for class assignments or debates, teachers and faculty seeking to supplement course materials, and others wanting to understand current issues better. By presenting how people in various countries perceive the root causes, current consequences, and proposed solutions to worldwide challenges, Global Viewpoints volumes offer readers opportunities to enhance their global awareness and their knowledge of cultures worldwide.

Introduction

> "We will spare no effort to free our fellow men, women and children from the abject and dehumanizing conditions of extreme poverty, to which more than a billion of them are currently subjected."
>
> —General Assembly,
> United Nations
> Millennium Declaration,
> September 8, 2000

No one would dispute that large numbers of people around the world live in poverty. But establishing a measurement for poverty, determining what causes poverty, and deciding how to reduce poverty are all issues with little consensus. The international community showed a certain degree of accord in establishing the Millennium Development Goals, the first of which is to eradicate extreme poverty and hunger. At the Millennium Summit in September 2000 the largest gathering of world leaders in history adopted the United Nations (UN) Millennium Declaration, committing their nations to a series of time-bound targets with a deadline of 2015 that have become known as the Millennium Development Goals. Even though there is fairly widespread agreement regarding the goal of eradicating extreme poverty, debate abounds on how to define poverty, extreme or otherwise.

Defining poverty, in order to measure it, is an issue that has prompted divergent views. Broadly speaking, poverty is the state of having a deficiency of basic necessities such as food, water, shelter, health care, and clothing. Exactly what level of deficiency of these items constitutes a state of poverty is debatable. One method of defining poverty is to develop a threshold based on income, where all those under a certain income amount are considered poor. For the purposes of the first Millennium Development Goal, the target set regarding poverty, is to "halve, between 1990 and 2015, the proportion of people whose income is less than $1 a day." This measurement based on income has been updated in the years since.

In 1993 the international poverty line for extreme poverty was defined at $1.08, based on the World Bank's $1-a-day measurement. To measure poverty in countries outside the United States, the US dollar amount is translated into local currency using the purchasing power parity of a certain group of basic goods, rather than currency exchange rates, in order to attempt to capture levels of purchasing power for similar basic goods. In 2005 the international extreme poverty line was updated by the World Bank to be defined as living on less than $1.25 per day (at 2005 prices, adjusted to account for the differences in purchasing power across countries). According to the World Bank, in 2005 there were 1.4 billion people in the developing world living on less than $1.25 a day and thus qualified as living in extreme poverty. This number amounts to over 20 percent of the world's population, but some say it is an arbitrary measure of poverty.

Setting the poverty line at $1.25, even adjusting for purchasing power, is an absolute method of measuring poverty. This absolute method of measuring poverty is most commonly used in developing countries. According to the $1.25-a-day measure, there is no extreme poverty in the United States, Canada, Australia, New Zealand, and the countries of Western Europe. However, developed countries tend to have their own national measure of poverty or one that defines poverty relative to the mean or median income in the country. For instance, the United States uses an absolute measure of poverty that was adopted in the mid-1960s and is adjusted each year for inflation. In 2010 the poverty line for one person under sixty-five years old was $11,344 per year, or just over $31 a day. The US poverty line is criticized by some for being too high and by others for being too low.

In contrast, the countries of the European Union (EU) measure those who are at risk of poverty as relative to median income, as does the Organisation for Economic Co-operation and Development (OECD). According to Eurostat, "The common threshold applied to at-risk-of-poverty indicators in the EU is that of 60% of median equivalised disposable income after social transfers." This means, however, that the poverty threshold varies widely among European countries as the median income varies widely. France, for example, had a poverty threshold of approximately €10,000 per year in 2007, or approximately $37 a day, whereas the poverty threshold for Portugal was approximately half of French poverty threshold.

The Oxford Poverty and Human Development Initiative (OPHI) has proposed the Multidimensional Poverty Index (MPI), which "complements income poverty measures by reflecting the deprivations that a poor person faces all at once with respect to education, health and living standard." The MPI uses ten indicators to measure education, health, and living standard as critical dimensions of poverty in developing countries. The MPI was developed in an attempt to not only measure poverty but also to gain knowledge on how people are poor in order to create more effective human development programs and policies.

It is clear to see that using the different poverty measures of various countries and organizations yields different answers to the question of who is poor. Coming to some agreement on how to define and measure poverty is important because it also impacts the related questions about the causes of poverty and the effective remedies for eradicating poverty. In looking at some of the numerous approaches to defining, understanding, and remedying poverty, various viewpoints from around the world are explored in *Global Viewpoints: Poverty*.

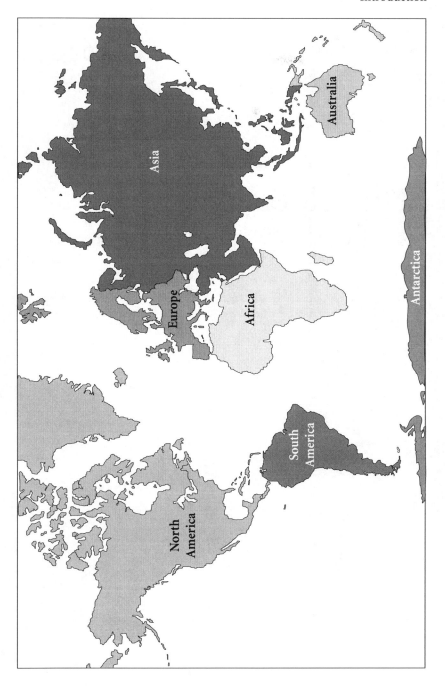

 GLOBALVIEWPOINTS

The Global Issue of Poverty

The Global Recession Has Caused a Slowdown in Progress Against Poverty

United Nations

In the following viewpoint, the United Nations contends that the global economic crisis slowed the first Millennium Development Goal of eradicating extreme poverty and hunger by 2015. Despite the slowdown, the United Nations claims that the target can still be met. The United Nations argues that progress continues to be stalled by slow job growth and continued hunger in the developing world. The United Nations is an international organization of countries committed to maintaining international peace and security; developing friendly relations among nations; and promoting social progress, better living standards, and human rights.

As you read, consider the following questions:

1. According to the United Nations, what two countries continue to have the sharpest reductions in poverty?
2. The author cites a study by the International Labour Organization showing what ratio of workers and their families worldwide were living in extreme poverty in 2009?

3. The proportion of children under age five who are underweight declined by how much between 1990 and 2009, according to the author?

Robust growth in the first half of the decade reduced the number of people in developing countries living on less than $1.25 a day from about 1.8 billion in 1990 to 1.4 billion in 2005. At the same time, the corresponding poverty rate dropped from 46 per cent to 27 per cent. The economic and financial crisis that began in the advanced countries of North America and Europe in 2008 sparked declines in commodity prices, trade and investment, resulting in slower growth globally.

Despite these declines, current trends suggest that the momentum of growth in the developing world remains strong enough to sustain the progress needed to reach the global poverty-reduction target. Based on recently updated projections from the World Bank, the overall poverty rate is still expected to fall below 15 per cent by 2015, indicating that the Millennium Development Goal (MDG) target can be met.

Progress on Poverty Reduction

The World Bank's new poverty projections for 2015 incorporate several changes: additional data from over 60 new household surveys, updates of historical consumption per capita from national accounts, and a new forecast of growth in per capita consumption. The forecast therefore captures changes in income distribution in countries for which new survey data are available and assumes that inequality remains unchanged in other countries. It also incorporates some of the effects of the global economic crisis, such as food and fuel price shocks. By 2015, the number of people in developing countries living on less than $1.25 a day is projected to fall below 900 million.

The fastest growth and sharpest reductions in poverty continue to be found in eastern Asia, particularly in China, where the poverty rate is expected to fall to under 5 per cent by 2015. India has also contributed to the large reduction in global poverty. In that country, poverty rates are projected to fall from 51 per cent in 1990 to about 22 per cent in 2015. In China and India combined, the number of people living in extreme poverty between 1990 and 2005 declined by about 455 million, and an additional 320 million people are expected to join their ranks by 2015. Projections for sub-Saharan Africa are slightly more upbeat than previously estimated. Based on recent economic growth performance and forecasted trends, the extreme poverty rate in the region is expected to fall below 36 per cent.

The task of monitoring progress on poverty reduction is beset by a lack of good quality surveys carried out at regular intervals, delays in reporting survey results, and insufficient documentation of country-level analytical methods used. It is also hampered by difficulties in accessing the underlying survey micro-data required to compute the poverty estimates. These gaps remain particularly problematic in sub-Saharan Africa, where the data necessary to make comparisons over the full range of MDGs are available in less than half the countries. For example, between 2007 and 2009, the countries that had collected, analysed and disseminated survey data, represent only 20 per cent of the region's population.

The Recovery in Employment

More than three years have passed since the onset of the fastest and deepest drop in global economic activity since the Great Depression. While global economic growth is rebounding, the global labour market is, in many respects, behaving as anticipated in the middle of the crisis: stubbornly elevated unemployment and slow employment generation in developed economies, coupled with widespread deficits in decent work in even the fastest-growing developing countries.

In the developed regions, the employment-to-population ratio dropped from 56.8 per cent in 2007 to 55.4 per cent in 2009, with a further drop to 54.8 per cent in 2010. Clearly, many developed economies are simply not generating sufficient employment opportunities to absorb growth in the working-age population. Again, this reflects an ongoing lag between economic recovery and a recovery in employment in this region. This contrasts with many developing regions, some of which saw an initial decline in the employment-to-population ratio but where, with the exception of the Caucasus [a geopolitical region at the border of Europe and Asia] and central Asia and eastern Asia, the estimated employment-to-population ratio in 2010 has changed little since 2007.

A slowdown in progress against poverty is reflected in the number of working poor.

In developing regions overall, the majority of workers are engaged in "vulnerable employment", defined as the percentage of own-account and unpaid family workers in total employment. Vulnerable employment is characterized by informal working arrangements, lack of adequate social protection, low pay and difficult working conditions.

On the basis of available data, it is estimated that the vulnerable employment rate remained roughly the same between 2008 and 2009, both in developing and developed regions. This compares with a steady average decline in the years preceding the economic and financial crisis. Increases in the vulnerable employment rate were found in sub-Saharan Africa and western Asia.

A slowdown in progress against poverty is reflected in the number of working poor. According to the International Labour Organization, one in five workers and their families worldwide were living in extreme poverty (on less than $1.25 per person per day) in 2009. This represents a sharp decline in poverty from a decade earlier, but also a flattening of the slope of the working poverty incidence curve beginning in 2007. The estimated rate for 2009 is 1.6 percentage points higher than the rate projected on the basis of the pre-crisis trend. While this is a crude estimate, it amounts to about 40 million more working poor at the extreme $1.25 level in 2009 than would have been expected on the basis of pre-crisis trends.

Hunger in the Developing World

The proportion of people in the developing world who went hungry in 2005–2007 remained stable at 16 per cent, despite significant reductions in extreme poverty. Based on this trend, and in light of the economic crisis and rising food prices, it will be difficult to meet the hunger-reduction target in many regions of the developing world.

The disconnect between poverty reduction and the persistence of hunger has brought renewed attention to the mechanisms governing access to food in the developing world. This year [2011], the Food and Agriculture Organization of the United Nations will undertake a comprehensive review of the causes behind this apparent discrepancy to better inform hunger-reduction policies in the future.

Trends observed in southeastern Asia, eastern Asia and Latin America and the Caribbean suggest that they are likely to meet the hunger-reduction target by 2015. However, wide disparities are found among countries in these regions. For example, the strong gains recorded in eastern Asia since 1990 are largely due to progress in China, while levels in southeastern Asia benefit from advances made in Indonesia and the Philippines. Based on current trends, sub-Saharan Africa will be unable to meet the hunger-reduction target by 2015.

Prevalence of Underweight Children

In developing regions, the proportion of children under age five who are underweight declined from 30 per cent to 23 per

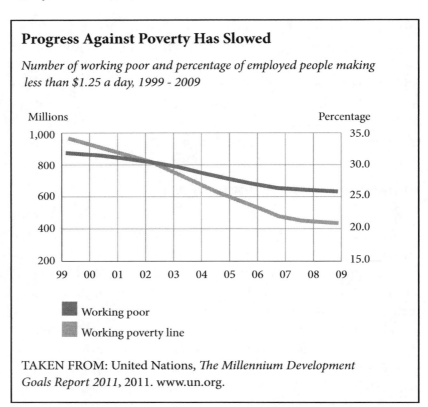

Progress Against Poverty Has Slowed

Number of working poor and percentage of employed people making less than $1.25 a day, 1999 - 2009

- ■ Working poor
- ■ Working poverty line

TAKEN FROM: United Nations, *The Millennium Development Goals Report 2011*, 2011. www.un.org.

cent between 1990 and 2009. Progress in reducing underweight prevalence was made in all regions where comparable trend data are available. Eastern Asia, Latin America and the Caribbean, and the Caucasus and central Asia have reached or nearly reached the MDG target, and southeastern Asia and northern Africa are on track.

However, progress in the developing regions overall is insufficient to reach the target by 2015. Children are underweight due to a combination of factors: lack of quality food, suboptimal feeding practices, repeated attacks of infectious diseases and pervasive undernutrition. In southern Asia, for example, one finds not only a shortage of quality food and poor feeding practices, but also a lack of flush toilets and other forms of improved sanitation. Nearly half the population practises open defecation, resulting in repeated bouts of diarrhoeal disease in children, which contribute to the high prevalence of undernutrition. Moreover, more than a quarter of infants in that region weigh less than 2,500 grams at birth. Many of these children are never able to catch up in terms of their nutritional status. All these factors conspire to make underweight prevalence in the region the highest in the world.

The poorest children are making the slowest progress in reducing underweight prevalence.

Nutrition must be given higher priority in national development if the MDGs are to be achieved. A number of simple, cost-effective measures delivered at key stages of the life cycle, particularly from conception to two years after birth, could greatly reduce undernutrition. These measures include improved maternal nutrition and care, breastfeeding within one hour of birth, exclusive breastfeeding for the first 6 months of life, and timely, adequate, safe, and appropriate complementary feeding and micronutrient intake between 6 and 24 months of age. Urgent, accelerated and concerted actions are needed to deliver and scale up such interventions to achieve MDG 1 and other health-related goals.

Children from the poorest households are more likely to be underweight than their richer counterparts. Moreover, the poorest children are making the slowest progress in reducing underweight prevalence. In southern Asia, for example, there was no meaningful improvement among children in the poorest households in the period between 1995 and 2009, while underweight prevalence among children from the richest 20 per cent of households decreased by almost a third.

Children in developing regions are twice as likely to be underweight if they live in rural rather than urban areas. Little difference was found in underweight prevalence between girls and boys.

Global Poverty Has Decreased in Recent Years, Especially in Asia

Laurence Chandy and Geoffrey Gertz

In the following viewpoint, Laurence Chandy and Geoffrey Gertz argue that the reduction in poverty around the world since 2005 is unprecedented and is poised to continue. Chandy and Gertz contend that the sharpest fall in poverty has been in Asia and the least progress in reducing poverty has been in sub-Saharan Africa. Chandy and Gertz claim that economic growth is the reason for the reduction in poverty worldwide. They conclude that even though the global economic crisis and global food crisis have slowed reduction in poverty to some degree, the fight against poverty is succeeding. Chandy is a fellow and Gertz a research analyst in the Global Economy and Development program at the Brookings Institution.

As you read, consider the following questions:

1. Chandy and Gertz predict that by 2015 the prevalence of extreme poverty could fall to under how many people?
2. The authors claim that from 2003 to 2008 developing countries' economies advanced by what percentage each year?

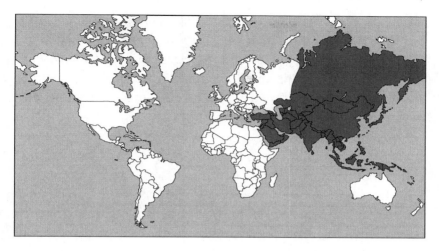

3. The bulk of the world's poor over the last thirty years has resided in what three areas, according to Chandy and Gertz?

To calculate the number of people in the world living in extreme poverty, we update the World Bank's official $1.25 a day poverty estimates for 119 countries, which together account for 95 percent of the population of the developing world. To do this, we take the most recent household survey data for each country, and generate poverty estimates for the years 2005 to 2015 using historical and forecast estimates of per capita consumption growth, making the simplifying assumption that the income distribution in each country remains unchanged. Global poverty figures are then calculated by adding together the number of poor from each country.

The Rapid Decline in Global Poverty

Our results indicate that the world has seen a dramatic decrease in global poverty over the past six years, and that this trend is set to continue in the four years ahead. We estimate that between 2005 and 2010, the total number of poor people around the world fell by nearly half a billion people, from over 1.3 billion in 2005 to under 900 million in 2010. Looking ahead to 2015, extreme poverty could fall to under 600 million people—less than half the number regularly cited in describing the number of poor people in the world today. Poverty reduction of this magnitude is unparalleled in history: Never before have so many people been lifted out of poverty over such a brief period of time.

When measured as a share of population, progress remains impressive, but is more in line with past trends. In the early 1980s, more than half of all people in developing countries lived in extreme poverty. By 2005, this was down to a quarter. According to our estimates, as of 2010 less than 16 percent remained in poverty, and fewer than 10 percent will likely be poor by 2015.

Poverty reduction of this magnitude is unparalleled in history: Never before have so many people been lifted out of poverty over such a brief period of time.

The first Millennium Development Goal defines a target (MDG1a) of halving the rate of global poverty by 2015 from its 1990 level. In an official report prepared for the U.N. [United Nations] MDG conference this past September [2010], the World Bank stated that we are 80 percent of the way toward this target and are on track to meet it by 2015, though the bank warned that "the economic crisis adds new risks to prospects for reaching the goal."

Our assessment is considerably more upbeat. We believe that the MDG1a target has already been met—approximately three years ago. Furthermore, by 2015, we will not only have halved the global poverty rate, as per MDG1a, but will have halved it again.

Over the past half century, the developing world, including many of the world's poorest countries, have seen dramatic improvements in virtually all non-income measures of well-being: Since 1960, global infant mortality has dropped by more than 50 percent, for example, and the share of the world's children enrolled in primary school increased from less than half to nearly 90 percent between 1950 and today. Likewise there have been impressive gains in gender equality, access to justice and civil and political rights. Yet, through most of this period, the incomes of rich and poor countries diverged, and income poverty has proven a more persistent challenge than other measures of well-being. The rapid decline in global poverty now under way—and the early achievement of the MDG1a target—marks a break from these trends, and could come to be seen as a turning point in the history of global development.

Poverty Reduction Around the World

Today's massive reduction in global poverty represents the aggregate of a number of individual regional and national success stories.

Unlike previous decades, like the '80s (when the poverty rate increased in Africa) and the '90s (when it increased in Latin America and the former Soviet Union), poverty reduction is currently taking place in all regions of the world. The sharpest fall in poverty is occurring in Asia. South Asia alone is expected to see a reduction in the number of its poor of more than 430 million over the 10-year period we study, representing a fall in its poverty rate of over 30 percentage points. East Asia already recorded a vast drop in poverty between 1980 and 2005, and this trend is continuing: A further 250 million people in the region are expected to escape poverty by 2015, two-thirds of whom have likely already done so.

Perhaps the greatest surprise, however, is the one taking place in sub-Saharan Africa. Between 1980 and 2005, the region's poverty rate had consistently hovered above 50 percent. Given the continent's high population growth, its number of poor rose steadily.

29

Regional Poverty, 2005 and 2010

	2005		2010	
	Number of poor (millions)	Poverty rate (% population)	Number of poor (millions)	Poverty rate (% population)
Europe and Central Asia	16.0	3.4%	8.4	1.8%
Middle East and North Africa	9.4	3.8%	6.7	2.5%
Latin America and Caribbean	45.0	8.4%	35.0	6.2%
East Asia	304.5	16.8%	140.4	7.4%
South Asia	583.4	40.2%	317.9	20.3%
Sub-Saharan Africa	379.5	54.5%	369.9	46.9%
World	1,337.8	25.7%	878.2	15.8%

TAKEN FROM: Laurence Chandy and Geoffrey Gertz, "Poverty in Numbers: The Changing State of Global Poverty from 2005 to 2015," Policy Brief 2011-01, Brookings Institution, January 2011.

The current period is different. For the first time, sub-Saharan Africa's poverty rate has fallen below 50 percent. The total number of poor people in the region is falling too, albeit slowly. Better still, by 2015, the poverty rate is expected to fall below 40 percent—a rate China did not achieve until the mid-90s.

The bulk of the fall in global poverty can be attributed to the two developing giants, India and China.

At the national level, 85 of the 119 countries in our model see the number of their poor decrease between 2005 and 2015. Fifty-eight countries record drops in their poverty rate of at least five percentage points. Countries home to some of the largest poor populations—such as Bangladesh, Ethiopia, Pakistan, Vietnam, Indonesia and Brazil—see tens of millions of their citizens escape poverty. A number of African countries in which poverty has long been persistent—including Nigeria, South Africa, Mozambique, Ghana and Tanzania—follow closely behind.

However, the bulk of the fall in global poverty can be attributed to the two developing giants, India and China. They alone are responsible for three-quarters of the reduction in the world's poor expected over the 10-year period. India sees over 360 million people escape poverty, a number equal to that of all other countries combined. Since 1999, India has been home to more poor people than any other country, but in 2015, this burden will be passed to Nigeria. China, for its part, enters the period having already experienced a dramatic drop in poverty, and with the goal of eliminating poverty within sight. By 2015, with a further 203 million reduction in its number of poor people, this objective will effectively be achieved.

The Drivers of Poverty Reduction

To what can we attribute this stunning performance in global poverty reduction? The explanation must start with growth, and more precisely with the rapid and sustained growth the developing world has enjoyed over the recent past.

As a group, developing economies mustered an average annual growth rate in the '80s and '90s of just 3.5 and 3.6 percent, respectively, barely above their population growth. Since the start of the new millennium, however, growth in the developing world has been considerably faster, well above that of advanced economies. From 2003 onwards, developing economies have expanded by more than 6 percent in every year except 2009, during the height of the Great Recession. And unlike advanced economies, which today appear destined for an extended period of below-average growth, developing countries bounced back quickly from the downturn. Growth is once again back above 6 percent and is expected to stay there through at least 2015.

Moreover, not only is the developing world as a whole growing quickly today, but key countries capable of altering global poverty figures are experiencing uncommon economic success.

Small developing countries have only a negligible effect on global poverty figures, no matter how quickly they grow. Thus, the emergence of the four Asian Tigers—Hong Kong, Singapore, South Korea and Taiwan—from the '60s to the '80s represented a remarkable economic breakthrough without shifting Asia's poverty profile. And Africa's most compelling growth success stories—Botswana, Mauritius, Seychelles, Cape Verde and Comoros, which have a collective population of under 5 million—have demonstrated Africa's development potential, but haven't made a dent in the continent's poverty figures.

Likewise, the growth trajectories of developing countries with large populations but few poor people bear little influence on global poverty. So when Russia and Iran—both among the 15 most highly populated developing countries—grew rapidly in the first half of the last decade, their strong performances barely budged global poverty aggregates.

In contrast, today growth is being driven by a number of big countries which are home to large poor populations. Between 2005 and 2015, India (current population of 1,233m), Bangladesh (169m), Vietnam (89m) and Ethiopia (87m) are each expected to grow by at least 6.3 percent per year, and in the process, each is likely to see a quarter of its population lifted out of poverty. Other developing giants such as China, Pakistan, Indonesia and Nigeria also record marked reductions in their poverty rates attributable to their strong economic performances.

It is evident from our findings that the negative effects of the Great Recession on poverty are overwhelmed by the positive effects of several years of high growth.

The Impact of Recent Crises

But what about the impact of the food and financial crises? The World Bank has warned that the spike in food prices of 2007–08 pushed an additional 100 million people worldwide below the international poverty line, yet this figure should be taken with a grain of salt. While in some countries the rise in food prices undoubtedly increased poverty, it is problematic to extrapolate from such results to the global impact of higher food prices, as effects will differ from country to country. The widely held view that higher food prices are an unmitigated bad for the world's poor is certainly not true, and indeed there is some evidence that in both India and China an increase in food prices would more likely lessen poverty.

Estimating the effect of the financial crisis and the subsequent growth slowdown on global poverty figures is a more straightforward exercise. The World Bank reports that due to the unexpected decline in developing country growth, the economic downturn of 2008–09 will keep an additional 64 million people in poverty. Our analysis accounts for the impact of the Great Recession on poverty, as our data include the lowered expectations of the post-crisis period; in other words, if not for the financial crisis our results would be even more dramatic than they are. Furthermore, it is evident from our findings that the negative effects of the Great Recession on poverty are overwhelmed by the positive effects of several years of high growth. 2009 marked one mediocre year of poverty reduction amidst a decade of extraordinary poverty reduction; why should the former receive so much attention and the latter so little?

The rapid growth of developing and emerging economies—including highly populated countries with large numbers of poor people—should no longer be news to anyone. The changing global economic balance has been the focus of countless best-selling books in recent years and has emerged as a dominant theme shaping how we view today's current affairs. Yet due to outdated poverty data, our sense of global poverty has not adapted to this narrative, and remains firmly stuck in the past. It is time we updated our conception of global poverty in line with our conception of today's global economy, as the two issues are inextricably linked.

Between 2005 and 2015, Asia's share of global poverty is expected to fall from two-thirds to one-third, while Africa's share more than doubles from 28 to 60 percent.

Global Poverty in the Future

While the vast majority of countries are showing at least some success in pulling their citizens out of poverty, the rate at which they are doing so varies considerably by continent, income level and degree of fragility. As a result, the global poverty landscape will dramatically change over the decade from 2005 to 2015.

For the past 30 years, the bulk of the world's poor—never less than 94 percent—has resided in three areas: East Asia, South Asia and sub-Saharan Africa. . . . With Asia's economic rise, however, its share of global poverty is falling sharply, leaving Africa responsible for a growing proportion of the world's poor. Between 2005 and 2015, Asia's share of global poverty is expected to fall from two-thirds to one-third, while Africa's share more than doubles from 28 to 60 percent. Poverty will thus increasingly be seen as an African problem, despite the clear progress the continent is now making.

While poverty is becoming more concentrated at a regional level, the opposite is true at a country level. In 2005, half the world's poor could be found in just two countries: India and China. By 2015, it is the top five countries, rather than the top two, that account for this share. Similarly, eight countries were home to three-quarters of the world's poor in 2005, compared to 15 countries in 2015. Six years ago, those interested in serving the preponderance of the world's poor could focus on just a handful of countries. By 2015, this will no longer be the case. . . .

In the span of a decade, the share of the world's population living in poverty could be cut by two-thirds.

The Fight Against Poverty

For many years, a debate raged amongst development academics, advocates and policy makers on the role of growth in poverty reduction and development, with some suggesting issues such as inequality and redistribution merited greater attention. Today, the development community has thankfully largely moved beyond this debate, with a broad consensus rightfully asserting the role of growth at the center of poverty alleviation.

This analytical evolution has happily coincided with a period of rapid economic growth in the developing world, even despite the setback of the Great Recession. The new estimates of global poverty presented in this brief serve as a reminder of just how powerful high growth can be in freeing people from poverty. In the span of a decade, the share of the world's population living in poverty could be cut by two-thirds, the number of countries where more than 1 in 6 people live in poverty could drop from 60 to 35, and 19 countries are poised to eliminate poverty altogether.

Of course, it is far too early to declare success in the fight against poverty. To begin with, our estimates are just that; they are not hard numbers that can be calculated in real time, and the gains we imagine might not be realized if projections of future consumption growth turn out to be overly optimistic or if the poor do not share in this growth. Moreover, even if our figures are broadly accurate, in 2015 there will still be close to 600 million people—twice the population of the United States—living on less than the meager sum of $1.25 a day. Their fates are far from secure and represent a strategic and moral failure for the rest of the world, arguably all the more so as millions of others escape poverty.

Nevertheless, the rate at which the developing world is now pulling people above the $1.25 threshold is tantalizing. The "dream of a world free of poverty," the oft-ridiculed motto emblazoned at the entrance of the World Bank, is, year by year, coming closer to reality.

Poverty Is Worsening in Many Countries, Especially in Sub-Saharan Africa

Nicholas N. Eberstadt

In the following viewpoint, Nicholas N. Eberstadt argues that despite the fact that the formula for prosperity is obvious, numerous countries around the globe are experiencing growing poverty rather than growing prosperity. Pointing to Haiti and sub-Saharan Africa as examples of countries that have experienced negative economic growth in previous years, Eberstadt contends that such socioeconomic failure is puzzling given the opportunities for economic advancement. Eberstadt suggests that issues of culture and governance are the primary causes of economic failure and concludes that the end of poverty in countries with poor governance is unlikely anytime soon. Eberstadt is the Henry Wendt Scholar in Political Economy at the American Enterprise Institute for Public Policy Research. He is the author of The Poverty of "The Poverty Rate": Measure and Mismeasure of Want in Modern America.

As you read, consider the following questions:

1. According to Eberstadt, an earthquake similar in strength to Haiti's 2010 earthquake occurred when and where?

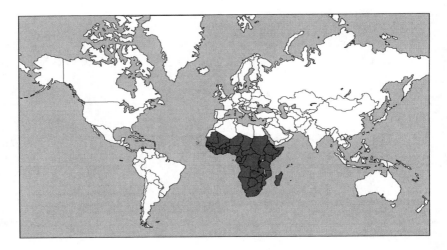

2. In how many countries, according to the author, was real per capita export revenue lower in 2007 than in 1980?

3. Eberstadt claims that what crucial issue is shaped by and independently shapes local attitudes, expectations, and motivations?

For a brief, glorious, and unforgettable moment 20 years ago, it seemed as if a great and terrible question that had been perennially stalking humanity had finally been answered. That profound question was as old as human hope itself: Could ordinary men and women, regardless of their location on this earth or their station in this life, hope that deliberate social arrangements could provide them—and their descendants thereafter—with permanent and universal protection against the grinding poverty and material misery that had been the human lot ever since memory began? For those exhilarating few years back in the 1990s, it seemed to many of us that the 20th century had indeed answered this age-old question: decisively, successfully, and conclusively.

The End of Poverty

Brute facts, after all, had demonstrated beyond controversy that human beings the world over could now indeed create sustained explosions of mass prosperity—rather than temporary and transient windfalls—that would utterly transform the human material condition, relegating the traditional conception of desperate want from a daily personal concern to an almost abstract textbook curiosity.

The plain and unavoidable truth is that countries with hundreds of millions of inhabitants today are not simply falling behind in a global march toward ever-greater prosperity: They are positively heading in the wrong direction.

According to estimates by the late economic historian Angus Maddison, the world's *average* per capita output quadrupled between 1900 and 1989/91, with even greater income surges registered in the collectivity of Western societies where the process of modern economic growth had commenced. Membership in this "Western" club, though, manifestly did not require European background or heritage, for the Asian nations of Japan, South Korea, and Taiwan had come to embrace political and economic arrangements similar to those pioneered in Western Europe and its overseas offshoots, and had in fact enjoyed some of the century's fastest rates of long-term income growth.

The formula for generating steady improvements in living standards for a diversity of human populations, in short, had been solidly established. The matter at hand was now to extend that formula to the reaches of the earth where it could not yet be exercised—most obviously at that time for political reasons, given the fact that nearly a third of the world's peoples were still living under Communist regimes in the late 1980s.

By the early 1990s, with the final failure of the Soviet project and the widely heralded idea of the "End of History," it suddenly seemed as if the liberal political ideals that promoted the spread of the Western growth formula would no longer encounter much organized global resistance. It now seemed only a matter of time until *every* part of the world could join in a newly possible economic race to the top. Prosperity for all—everywhere—no longer sounded like merely a prayer. Quite the contrary: The end of global poverty was increasingly taken to be something much more like a feasible long-term-action agenda.

Alas, in the years since, new brute facts have asserted themselves, while other awkward facts of somewhat older vintage have reasserted themselves, demanding renewed attention. All too many contemporary locales have managed to "achieve" records of long-term economic failure in our modern era. The plain and unavoidable truth is that countries with hundreds of millions of inhabitants today are not simply falling behind in a global march toward ever-greater prosperity: They are positively heading in the wrong direction, spiraling down on their own distinct, but commonly dismal, paths of severe, prolonged, and tragic retrogression.

The Earthquake in Haiti

Haiti is a particularly awful case in point.

Conditions of life in Haiti, wretched for most Haitians even in the best of times, took a sharp turn for the worse earlier this year [2010], when an earthquake measuring 7.0 on the Richter scale struck not far from the capital of Port-au-Prince. The resultant carnage was heartrending; the chaos, stomach-churning. At this writing, the official estimate of the death toll from the disaster has risen above 200,000—although it is a telling sign of Haiti's sheer underdevelopment that an exact death count from the earthquake and its aftermath is regarded by foreign relief workers on the scene as an utterly unrealistic proposition.

Yet there was absolutely nothing "natural" about the human cost of this natural disaster. Massive earthquakes do not always unfold as calamities of biblical proportions, even when they are visited on major urban population centers. In October 1989, a massive earthquake suddenly struck the Bay Area of California. In sheer magnitude, that earthquake was almost as violent as Haiti's (6.9 vs. 7.0); its epicenter was roughly as far from downtown San Jose as Haiti's was from central Port-au-Prince. The final death toll in the Bay Area tragedy: 63 lives.

At first glance, such wildly disparate death counts in the face of arguably comparable natural calamities may seem to serve as a grim metaphor for the seemingly perennial yawning gap that separates life chances in rich and poor regions today. In reality, however, the backstory is still sadder than these raw numbers might of themselves suggest: For the awful fact of the matter is that the United States and Haiti are societies whose capabilities for meeting human needs (and protecting human beings) have been moving in fundamentally different directions for decades.

Negative Economic Growth

A society's material capabilities for meeting human needs are very broadly indicated by its levels and trends in per capita output (GDP [gross domestic product]). America is not one of the modern world's most rapidly growing economies—over the past century, in fact, per capita growth has averaged a little under 2 percent a year—but thanks to the power of compound interest, such a tempo of growth brings dramatic and salutary transformations over time, if it can be sustained. In the roughly six decades between 1950 and 2008, indeed, America's per capita output more than tripled. But over that same half century or so, by Maddison's reckoning, per capita output in Haiti actually *declined*—by more than a third.

Thanks to its prolonged economic retrogression, Haiti to-day is not simply immiserated; it is in fact substantially poorer than it was half a century ago. By the hardly insignificant yardstick of income levels, the country appears to be *less* developed now than it was two generations before. (Appalling death tolls in the face of earthquakes, tropical storms, and other forces of nature are merely one manifestation of the more general deterioration in material capabilities for meeting human needs that are implied by such trends.)

Haiti, moreover, is only one of many countries in the modern world to have been heading down—not up—in economic terms for decades on end. Summary statistics from the World Bank and the World Trade Organization (WTO) outline the dimensions of this global problem.

By the World Bank's calculations, nearly two dozen countries suffered negative per capita economic growth over the course of the quarter century from 1980 to 2005. And the World Bank does not even attempt to estimate economic trends for a number of national problem cases—Kim Jong-il's North Korea and Robert Mugabe's Zimbabwe among them— where pronounced and prolonged economic decline have almost certainly taken place. When one tallies up the global totals, it would appear that close to half a billion people today live in such countries—societies beset not merely by long-term stagnation but also by a quarter century or more of absolute deterioration in income levels.

Hundreds of millions of people in the modern world live in places where the development process is manifestly stuck in reverse.

Prolonged Economic Failure

At the same time, WTO numbers point to a jarring drop in the long-term export performance of many contemporary societies. Adjusting for inflation, these WTO data suggest that more than 30 countries were actually earning in real terms less from merchandise exports in 2006 than they did in 1980, over a quarter century earlier. The picture is still worse when we take intervening population growth into account. Real per capita export revenue, measured in U.S. dollars, looks to have been lower in more than 50 countries in 2007 (the last year before the current worldwide economic crisis) than in 1980. In all, such places today account for roughly three-quarters of a billion of the world's 6.8 billion current inhabitants—about a ninth of the globe's total population.

Thus, it is not just that an appreciable swath of humanity today lives in countries that have not yet managed to customize, and apply, the global formula for sustained growth that has been propelling the rest of the world out of poverty and into material security, or even affluence. No—hundreds of millions of people in the modern world live in places where the development process is manifestly stuck in reverse.

For these hapless societies, pronounced and relentless economic failure is not an awful aberration but rather the seemingly "natural" way of things: the only way things have ever been in living memory for most locals, and most international observers. After all, the median age of the world's present population is less than 30 years; this means that most people today can recall only long-term economic failure for these dozens of countries.

National examples of prolonged economic failure dot the modern global map: in the Caribbean (Cuba, Haiti); in Latin America (Paraguay, Venezuela); even in dynamic East Asia (North Korea). But the epicenter of prolonged economic failure is sub-Saharan Africa.

The Case of Sub-Saharan Africa

Sub-Saharan Africa comprises an extraordinary diversity of peoples, and the economic records of each of the region's 50-

plus countries is separate and distinct. Yet taken together, their overall development record in the post-colonial period has been utterly dismal.

Some improvement in the region's economic performance has been registered since the mid-1990s. Even so, according to estimates by both Angus Maddison and the World Bank, per capita income for the region as a whole was slightly lower in 2006 than it was in 1974. Much the same holds true for real per capita export earnings. According to the WTO's numbers, Africa's overall per capita merchandise export revenues, adjusted for inflation, showed absolutely no improvement between 1974 and 2006—and after the global economic crisis, they appear to have been around 10 percent *lower* in 2009 than they were in 1974.

This is very bad news for a very large number of people: As of last year, according to U.S. Census Bureau projections, sub-Saharan Africa's population was well over 800 million people, roughly one-eighth of all human beings on earth today. . . .

The Puzzling Problem of Socioeconomic Failure

The problem of sustained socioeconomic retrogression is all the more dismaying, and puzzling, when one bears in mind the phenomenal explosion of prosperity that has transformed the world as a whole in the modern era—and the potentialities for material advance that are afforded even the poorest societies.

In the half century between 1955 and 2005, by Maddison's reckoning, the planet's per capita income levels nearly tripled, growing at an average tempo of more than 2 percent per year, despite the unprecedented pace of population increase in the Third World over those same years. The expansion of international trade—and thus by definition, of markets for export produce—was even more dramatic: On a worldwide basis, real per capita demand for international merchandise and commodities jumped almost tenfold during those same years. . . .

So, given the pervasive scope and scale of worldwide economic advance in our age—and the apparently increasing ease of achieving sustained economic progress, even for populations at the lowest levels of material attainment—how are we to explain, and deal with, the phenomenon of persisting socioeconomic failure in Haiti and dozens of other contemporary societies? How have these places managed to avoid self-enrichment, given the apparently increasing worldwide odds against such an outcome? And what can be done to end the syndrome of developmental decline on the lands that have been subject to it?. . .

The problem of sustained socioeconomic retrogression is all the more dismaying, and puzzling, when one bears in mind the phenomenal explosion of prosperity that has transformed the world as a whole in the modern era.

Culture and Governance

The proposition that a local population's viewpoints, values, and dispositions might have some bearing on local economic performance would hardly seem to be controversial. Decades ago, the great development economist Peter Bauer wrote that "economic achievement depends upon a people's attributes, attitudes, mores and political arrangements." The observation was offered as a simple and irrefutable statement of fact, and it would still be unobjectionable today to most readers who have not been tutored in contemporary "development theory." But for development specialists, discussion of "culture"— much less its relationship to such things as work, thrift, savings, entrepreneurship, innovation, educational attainment, and other qualities that influence prospects for material advance—is increasingly off-limits.

In the erudite reaches of development policy, indeed, discussion of such matters at all is often regarded as poor form at best—and at worst is taken to smack of condescension, paternalism, or even latent prejudice. Paul Collier's best-selling 2007 exposition, *The Bottom Billion*, is a case in point. Remarkably, Collier manages to complete his opus without ever referring to cultural impediments to economic progress in the world's poorest and most economically stagnant societies. In fact, he utters the word *culture* only once—and that once as a reference to the contending worldviews and approaches of various parties involved in international-aid negotiations.

To be sure, the record of historical efforts to predict and explain economic performance on the basis of cultural attributes is, let us say, checkered. Up through the 1950s and even into the early 1960s, for example, researchers and self-styled experts were offering confident and detailed explanations of why "Confucian values" constituted a serious obstacle to economic development in East Asia. A decade or so later— after the huge boom all around the East Asian rim was well under way—the profession was still united in the consensus that the Confucian ethos mattered greatly in economic performance, but they had quietly shifted their estimate of that impact from negative to positive.

This gets us to the crucial issue of governance—which is shaped by, and in turn independently shapes, local attitudes, expectations, and motivations. Throughout the reaches of the world characterized by long-term economic failure, governance has generally been abysmal. Violent political instability and predatory, arbitrary, or plainly destructive state practices have shaken, or sometimes altogether destroyed, the institutions and legal rules upon which purposeful individual and collective efforts for economic betterment depend. In a few spots on the map—such as North Korea—pronounced economic failure is due to "strong states": monster regimes that starve their subjects as a matter of principle or ideology, given their own twisted official logic. For many more of today's failed economies, the trouble instead is that governance has been the charge of "weak" states or even "failed states": polities with extremely fragile capabilities, sometimes lacking the ability to maintain order or guarantee their subjects' physical security at all (think Liberia, Sierra Leone, Somalia). . . .

Throughout the reaches of the world characterized by long-term economic failure, governance has generally been abysmal.

The Possibilities of Prosperity for All

On the one hand, the formula for achieving sustained long-term economic growth on a national basis has pretty clearly been developed, if not perfected—and applying this formula looks to be easier than ever before in human history. Most people, moreover, live in countries that have accepted the arrangements to undergird this growth formula—some by deliberately and enthusiastically embracing them, others by more inadvertently stumbling upon them. Barring global catastrophe—some unforeseen worldwide conflagration or environmental debacle—these populations in general can expect their descendants to enjoy higher incomes and greater affluence than they themselves have ever known. Moreover, thanks to what the economic historian Alexander Gerschenkron described as "the advantages of backwardness," untapped technological and economic potentialities provide the poorer populations in this group with the possibilities of even more rapid growth than those facing the richer world.

On the other hand, many hundreds of millions of people—a fraction of humanity that may rise, not fall, in the years immediately ahead—cannot avail themselves of the basic political arrangements that set the global growth formula into action. For now, and for the foreseeable future, these *mis-*

erables can look forward only to relative economic decline—or even further absolute decline, difficult as that may be to imagine.

Nearly half a century ago, Peter Bauer warned presciently that "if attitudes, mores and institutions uncongenial to material progress have prevailed for long historical periods, with corresponding effects on material advance, it may be difficult to reverse their effects except after long periods." We are living in the world Bauer prophesied. Global prosperity for all is not yet at hand—and, painful and indeed shocking as this may be to recognize, the day in which *all* humanity can expect to be included in the march toward ever greater affluence cannot be foreseen with any confidence.

Most of the World's Poor Now Live in Middle-Income Countries

Andy Sumner

In the following viewpoint, Andy Sumner maintains that the poor people in middle-income countries are being overlooked because of a focus on poor countries rather than poor people. Sumner claims that the majority of poor people no longer live in low-income countries, as was the case a couple decades ago, but now live in middle-income countries. He cautions that development policy needs to take this shift into account so that it does not leave the poor in middle-income countries behind. Sumner is a research fellow in the Vulnerability and Poverty Reduction Team at the Institute of Development Studies in the United Kingdom and a visiting fellow at the Center for Global Development in Washington, DC.

As you read, consider the following questions:

1. According to Sumner, the percentage of global poverty accounted for by middle-income countries, minus China and India, has recently increased by what factor?
2. Sumner suggests that rather than aiming development policy at poor countries, it should be aimed at what?

Andy Sumner, "The New Bottom Billion and the MDGs—A Plan of Action," *IDS In Focus Policy Briefing*, vol. 16, no. 1, October 2010, pp. 1–2.

3. According to the author, will most of the poor people in 2015 live in low-income countries or middle-income countries?

Popular understandings of global poverty are based on the false premise that poor people all live in poor countries. In fact, new estimates by the Institute of Development Studies place three-quarters of the world's 1.3bn [billion] or so poor people in middle-income countries (MICs) such as India, China, Nigeria, Pakistan and Indonesia, and only a quarter live in low-income countries (LICs), largely in Africa. This is a dramatic change from just two decades ago when 93 per cent of poor people lived in low-income countries. This change has major implications for both the achievement of the Millennium Development Goals (MDGs) and global strategies for poverty reduction beyond 2015.

Different Types of Poverty

If development is about poverty reduction, where poor people live is a crucial question. A host of countries have recently graduated to middle-income country status, but poor people within them are being left behind. This is not just about India and China, because the percentage of global poverty accounted for by the MICs minus China and India has tripled as a proportion of the global total. Further, this is not just about income poverty. The picture holds across nutrition MDG measures (children's height and weight) and the United Nations Development Programme's (UNDP's) new multidimensional poverty index. Where there is a nuance is if we look at the primary schooling MDG—and possibly the infant mortality MDG too—then, approximately 40 per cent of the poorest are still in low-income countries. We see a pattern reflecting different types of poverty in different places.

How did we work this out? We took the poverty and population data in the World Bank's World Development Indicators from 1988–1990 and 2007–2008 and estimated the number of millions of poor people for every country that had data. These estimates of actual millions of poor people are hidden in poverty percentages often used for MDG assessments. As the World Bank noted in the last systematic estimation by [Shaohua] Chen and [Martin] Ravallion (2008), there were actually more poor Africans and Indians than there were in 1990 even though as a percentage of the population poverty has fallen. Why have we only just 'discovered' this? Data are usually 2–4 years old and many of these countries have graduated in the last five years or so.

Policy Implications of the New Bottom Billion

1. A new focus on relative poverty should shape the aid agenda

Development policy needs to be about poor *people*, not just poor *countries*. We need to ask what aid is for in a LIC or MIC. We need a clear new commitment to reduce relative poverty and thus inequality and in doing so develop a broader range of catalytic aid instruments. These would seek to build emancipation from aid, want and insecurity by a new focus on relative poverty and supporting the expansion of the tax-paying middle classes. This would help to build the domestic tax system and improve governance and accountability.

Development policy needs to be about poor people, *not just poor* countries.

---

2. Tailor aid to LICs and MICs so that poverty is targeted wherever it occurs

Poverty may be increasingly turning from an international to a national distribution problem, potentially making governance and domestic taxation and redistribution policies more important than official development assistance (ODA). But this does not mean we should stop giving aid to 'poor

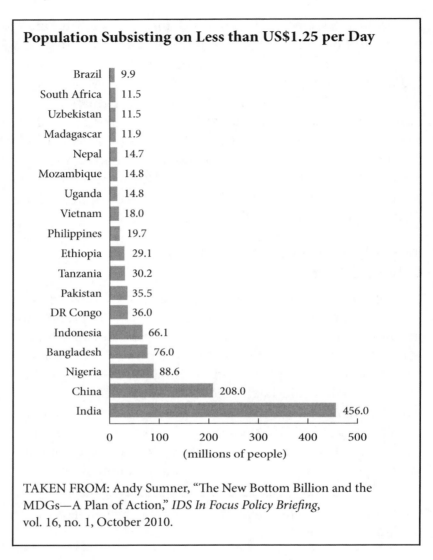

Population Subsisting on Less than US$1.25 per Day

Country	millions of people
Brazil	9.9
South Africa	11.5
Uzbekistan	11.5
Madagascar	11.9
Nepal	14.7
Mozambique	14.8
Uganda	14.8
Vietnam	18.0
Philippines	19.7
Ethiopia	29.1
Tanzania	30.2
Pakistan	35.5
DR Congo	36.0
Indonesia	66.1
Bangladesh	76.0
Nigeria	88.6
China	208.0
India	456.0

(millions of people)

TAKEN FROM: Andy Sumner, "The New Bottom Billion and the MDGs—A Plan of Action," *IDS In Focus Policy Briefing*, vol. 16, no. 1, October 2010.

countries'. Instead, donors need to differentiate more; the impact of the post-financial crisis on public revenues and spending means that LICs around the world need aid resources more than ever before. Although some MICs can support their own poor people, others cannot. Some are only just past the threshold and withdrawing aid suddenly might mean they slip back to LICs. Even when domestic resources appear more substantial, political will may be ambivalent. So in MICs the donor strategy should include a broader range of aid instruments beyond resources—for example, focusing on issues such as trade, migration and climate change.

3. A mechanism is needed that shares financial responsibility between richer and poorer countries

The donor community will have to choose how to respond to the New Bottom Billion. Increasingly, poverty reduction strategies and the global effort to reach the MDG targets will be as much about tackling inequality in MICs as it will be about an absolute lack of resources in the poorest countries. We need an approach which looks to poor people, wherever they live, and focuses on new partnerships between governments based on shared responsibility and accountability to the poor (such as the Responsibility to Protect, known as R2P in humanitarian situations) rather than a straightforward donor and recipient view of the world. This could work as a commitment to provide a minimum level of income, health care, and education for citizens, with the financial responsibility shared between rich and poor countries on a sliding scale depending on the wealth of the country where groups of poor people are living. However, the new MICs may well not want traditional development assistance. This would mean that donors would have to accept a move away from traditional aid to broad support for instruments that only indirectly benefit the poor in MICs.

According to the World Bank, there will be almost one billion poor people in 2015, even if the MDGs are met. Most of those remaining poor people will be in MICs and will be the very poorest or the 'hardest to reach' of all, as UNICEF [the United Nations Children's Fund] has noted. As debates start on a post-MDG framework with a view to the September 2013 UN high-level summit, new approaches will be needed. Any new global agreement needs to pay attention to the changing nature of global poverty as well as difficult issues such as climate change and adaptation, demography and urbanisation. The New Bottom Billion raises a very different set of challenges for policy makers in the run-up to 2015 from those they faced during the run-up to 2000 and the adoption of the Millennium Declaration.

Income Inequality and Relative Poverty Have Risen in Industrialized Countries

Organisation for Economic Co-operation and Development (OECD)

In the following viewpoint, the Organisation for Economic Co-operation and Development (OECD) contends that both inequality of income and poverty have increased in OECD member countries over the last twenty years. The size of the income inequality and the extent of relative poverty vary widely among developed countries, but the vast majority has experienced increases in both, argues the OECD. The OECD claims that changes in the employment market caused the growth in income inequality and concludes that countries should address inequality through policies that promote better employment rather than through higher social spending. OECD is a membership organization consisting of thirty-four advanced and emerging countries dedicated to global development.

As you read, consider the following questions:

1. According to the OECD, in what four OECD countries do more than 90 percent of the population agree that inequality is too great?

Organisation for Economic Co-operation and Development (OECD), Based on OECD (2008), "Are We Growing Unequal? New Evidence on Changes in Poverty and Incomes over the Past 20 Years," OECD Media Brief, October 2008. www.oecd.org/els/social /inequality/GU. Reproduced by permission.

2. The author claims that whereas the risk of poverty for older people in OECD countries has fallen, it has risen for what demographic?

3. Which four OECD countries spent 2 percent or less of national income on social spending benefits, according to the author?

The gap between rich and poor in most OECD [Organisation for Economic Co-operation and Development] countries has widened over the past two decades. This risks leaving more people behind in an ever-changing world economy. But the trend to greater inequality is not inevitable: Governments can close the gap with effective social policies, many of which do not need more social spending.

Inequality of incomes was higher in most OECD countries in the mid-2000s than in the mid-1980s. Only a few bucked the trend: France, Greece and Spain moved towards greater equality of incomes over the past 20 years.

This phenomenon continues: The past five years [2003–2008] saw growing poverty and inequality in two-thirds of OECD countries. Canada, Germany, Norway and the United States are the most affected. The remaining third—particularly Greece, Mexico and the United Kingdom—have seen a shrinking gap between rich and poor since 2000. This proves that there is nothing inevitable about these changes.

Income Inequality and Poverty

Many people in OECD countries are worried about these trends. In Japan, two-thirds of the population think that inequality is too great, while 90% or more of people agree in Hungary, Italy, Portugal and the Slovak Republic.

Politicians, across the whole spectrum, are also concerned. For example, George [W.] Bush, president of the United States, said in 2007, 'our citizens worry about the fact that our dynamic economy is leaving working people behind'. He added, 'Income inequality is real; it's been rising for more than 25 years'.

Inequality of incomes raises both political and economic challenges. Politically, income inequality can fuel populist and protectionist sentiments. Also, societies with a large gap between rich and poor face the threat of political power being confined to the hands of a few wealthy citizens.

The economic price of greater income inequality is the waste of human resources implied by a large portion of the population out of work but able to work or trapped in low-paid, low-skilled jobs.

But inequality is not just about income: It is about both *opportunities* and *outcomes*. Publicly provided services, such as education, health and housing, can also create fairer societies. There are still starker differences in financial assets between rich and poor than there are in income. Also, a low income for short periods (between jobs, say) is less hard on people than persistent poverty. . . .

The Gap Between Rich and Poor

The income of the richest 10% of people is, on average across OECD countries, nearly nine times that of the poorest 10%. But the size of income differentials varies. In Mexico, the richest have incomes of more than 25 times those of the poorest and, in Turkey, the ratio is 17 to one. The income gap between rich and poor is also well above the OECD average in Portugal, Poland and the United States.

But in Nordic countries, such as Denmark, Sweden and Finland, the gap is much smaller. The incomes of the richest 10% average around five times those of the poorest 10%.

A number of countries are bunched together around the OECD average. This group comprises most of the English-speaking countries (Canada and the United Kingdom, for example) and some southern European nations, such as Greece, Italy and Spain.

On average, the poorest 10% of the population have incomes of US$7,000 a year or less in OECD countries. This figure tends to be highest in Europe: averaging nearly US$8,000 compared with less than US$6,000 in the United States. It is much lower in the less-developed OECD economies: Just US$1,000 in Mexico and US$1,300 in Turkey. These differences are not surprising: General living standards are lower in these countries than elsewhere in the OECD.

But it does not follow that poor people in rich countries are always better off than their counterparts in lower income countries. For example, the poorest 10% in Sweden have incomes 1.5 times the level of the poorest 10% in the United States even though average incomes are higher there.

The income of the richest 10% of people is, on average across OECD countries, nearly nine times that of the poorest 10%.

The Prevalence of Poverty

It is important to remember that 'poverty' is a relative concept in developed economies. The comparison of incomes between countries shows, for example, that the poorest 10% in the United Kingdom have more money than the average Portuguese person. But what matters is the standard of living relative to other people in the country. Here, poverty is measured against prevalent national living standards, as measured by the median household income. This benchmark, of course, also varies over time.

Around one person in 10 in OECD countries had an income below half of the national median in 2005. But this differs hugely between countries: from one in 20 in Denmark to one in five in Mexico. Relative poverty rates are also low in the Czech Republic and Sweden. Poor people make up around 17% of the population in Turkey and the United States and 15% in Spain.

Countries with a wide distribution of income tend to have more widespread income poverty. But measures of inequality and poverty do not necessarily go hand in hand. In the English-speaking countries, income inequality is above the OECD average. However, poverty rates are above average in Australia, Canada, Ireland and the United States, about average in New Zealand but significantly below average in the United Kingdom.

An Increase in Inequality and Poverty

Both income inequality and relative poverty have risen over the past 20 years. The rise has been significant and widespread, affecting more than three-quarters of OECD countries.

The income gap between the richest 10% and the poorest 10% has grown. Other, more sophisticated, measures of income inequality were 7–8% higher in the mid-2000s than they were in the mid-1980s.

This may not sound like much of an increase, but it is equivalent on average to taking $880 away from the poorest 50% and giving $880 to the richest 50%, although incomes at every level grew over the two decades.

Both income inequality and relative poverty have risen over the past 20 years.

The poor population—with incomes below half the national median—grew by 1.3 percentage points, from 9.3% to 10.6% of the population in OECD countries.

These trends, however, have not been universal. The two poorest and most unequal OECD countries—Mexico and Turkey—saw substantial increases in inequality between the mid-1980s and mid-1990s. But there were equally substantial falls in the subsequent decade. In the United Kingdom, inequality increased significantly throughout the 1980s, then remained stable, and fell in the period 2000–05.

Where inequality increased, it was usually due to rich households faring much better than low-income families. But in some countries—such as Canada, Finland, Germany, Italy, Norway and the United States—the rich also gained ground on middle earners.

The most substantial shifts in poverty over the past two decades are between age groups. The risk of poverty for older people has fallen, while poverty of young adults and families with children has risen.

The over 75s remain the age group most likely to be poor, but the risk has fallen from nearly double the population average in the mid-1980s to 1.5 times higher in the mid-2000s. People aged 66–75 are now no more likely to be poor as the population as a whole.

Conversely, children and young adults have poverty rates that are now around 25% higher than the population average, while they were below or close to that average 20 years ago. And single-parent households are three times as likely to be poor as average. This disadvantage increased slightly between the mid-1990s and mid-2000s, albeit at a slow rate.

The Causes of Income Inequality

All OECD countries are undergoing a demographic transition, meaning fewer babies and longer lives. The result is more older people—at greater risk of poverty than the average—and fewer people of working age—with relatively low poverty risk. There are also many more single parents.

Yet these changes in demography and living arrangements, although profound, are not the main driver of changes in income distribution. They account for more than 20% of the increase in income inequality only in Australia, Canada, France, Germany, the Netherlands and the United Kingdom.

Developments in the labour market are the main origin of the changes in incomes. This is because earnings make up more than 70% of household incomes (before taxes). With a few exceptions, the disparity between the low- and high-paid has increased rapidly since the early 1990s. Usually, this was because the high-paid did particularly well, not only relative to low earners but also to middle earners.

However, there are now more people in work in most OECD countries. Family incomes are mostly higher when people are in rather than out of work.

With a few exceptions, the disparity between the low-and high-paid has increased rapidly since the early 1990s.

These two effects—more jobs, greater earnings inequality—offset one another to an extent. The rise in inequality of earnings between households has generally been less than growth in the pay gap between individuals.

Yet, there remains persistent joblessness, particularly among the low-skilled and those with few educational qualifications. Much of the increase in employment is from second earners in a household taking a job rather than people in jobless households finding work.

Employment and Poverty

Paid work reduces the risk of poverty: 46% of single people without work have low incomes, compared with 28% who work part-time and 8% of those working full-time. The same is true of couples: One in three has an income below the poverty line when both do not work. This proportion is only 19% when one of them has a job and just 4% when both partners work.

However, there is no guarantee that more jobs mean fewer poor people. Japan and the United States, for example, have both high employment rates and above-average poverty. In Hungary, the position is the opposite: a relatively low share of people in jobs but also rather a low poverty rate.

As earnings have become more unequal, so has income from capital: dividends, interest, rent, capital gains and so on. The distribution of self-employment incomes has also widened. Together, these changes account for a significant part of the growth in inequality of household income.

Inequality of market incomes (from earnings, self-employment, capital, etc.) increased more rapidly than that for net incomes (including benefits, for example) between the mid-1980s and the mid-2000s.

Dealing with Inequality and Poverty

Government plays a big role in determining incomes and living standards through the taxes it levies and the benefits it pays out.

In the Nordic countries, benefits and taxes are highly redistributive: taking money from the rich and giving it to the poor. Tax-and-benefit systems are also redistributive in Korea and the United States, but to a much lesser degree.

On average across OECD countries, cash transfers and income taxes reduce inequality by one-third. Poverty is around 60% lower than it would be without taxes and benefits. Even among the working-age population, government redistribution reduces poverty by about 50%.

Nevertheless, the impact of taxes and benefits on both poverty and inequality has fallen in the past ten years in many OECD countries. . . .

It makes a big difference to individuals whether low income is just for a short period (as a student or between jobs) or poverty is persistent or even permanent. Other people may have recurrent spells of low income.

In most OECD countries, around half of poor people are better off and move above the poverty line within three years. This figure is the highest in Denmark and the Netherlands. Income mobility means that people who are persistently poor make up less than 2% of the population in these two countries. But persistent poverty is much more widespread—7% of the population—in Australia, Greece, Ireland, Portugal and the United States.

Generally, the countries with more widespread poverty based on annual incomes tend also to have more people who are persistently poor. . . .

The Impact of Public Policies

Incomes are more equally distributed . . . and fewer people are poor where social spending is high: the Nordic countries and western European countries, such as Austria, Belgium and the Netherlands. Social spending on people of working age was 7–8% of national income in 2005 and the share of working-age people in poverty was between 5% and 8%.

At the other end of the spectrum, Korea, Mexico, Turkey and the United States spent 2% or less of national income on benefits and had 12–15% of the working-age population in poverty.

It is easy to conclude that countries have the poverty rate that they are prepared to pay for. In Mexico and Turkey, higher tax revenues—enabling an expansion of social programmes—would probably reduce inequality and poverty. But for most OECD countries, the answer is more complex.

Higher social spending does not always reduce poverty and inequality.

In Canada, for example, total social expenditure (including spending on older people) increased from 16% to 21% of national income in the early 1990s but by the early 2000s had

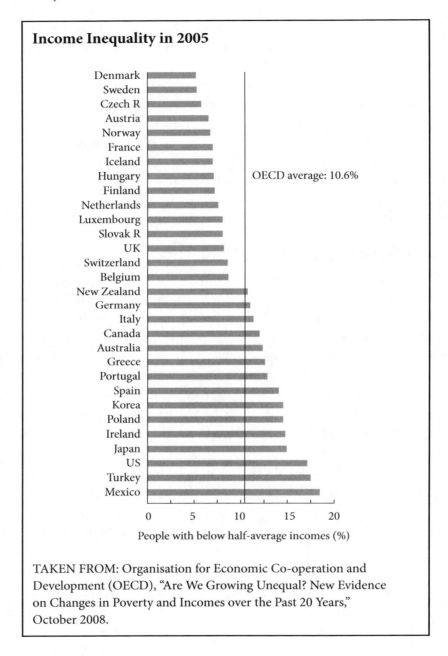

Income Inequality in 2005

OECD average: 10.6%

People with below half-average incomes (%)

TAKEN FROM: Organisation for Economic Co-operation and
Development (OECD), "Are We Growing Unequal? New Evidence
on Changes in Poverty and Incomes over the Past 20 Years,"
October 2008.

fallen back to 16% again. Over that period, a fairly constant
9–10% of the population was below the poverty line. In the

Netherlands, stable public social spending went hand in hand with significant growth in poverty between the mid-1980s and mid-1990s. But after that point, social spending fell from 27% to 20% of national income while the poverty rate remained constant. In contrast, fairly stable social spending of around 28% of national income in Germany in the 1990s and 2000s was accompanied by significantly greater poverty: increasing from around 7% of the population to nearly 12%.

Higher social spending does not always reduce poverty and inequality. And the taxes needed to pay for it could have the perverse effect of pricing people out of work. Instead, within current budgets, more effective policies could address the cause of growing inequality more directly.

Demographic and social changes that drive greater inequality and poverty are largely inevitable and beyond the power of governments to affect. However, the cause of much of growing inequality lies in the labour market: a larger gap between the low- and high-paid and changing numbers of people out of work. These are much more amenable to public policies, such as education and training to improve skills and in-work benefits that provide a financial incentive to take a job.

The Current Measure of Poverty Is Inadequate

David Woodward

In the following viewpoint, David Woodward argues that the existing poverty line utilized for the purposes of the Millennium Development Goals is an unreliable measure of poverty. Woodward claims that only looking at incomes and purchasing power parity creates arbitrary outcomes. He proposes a new approach to measuring poverty that takes account of indicators that reflect economic and social rights, such as health, nutrition, and education, that he calls the Rights-Based Poverty Line. Woodward is an economist and researcher on development issues in the Netherlands and was previously a fellow of the London-based New Economics Foundation.

As you read, consider the following questions:

1. According to Woodward, why is the dollar-a-day poverty line problematic?

2. The poverty line is updated on the basis of what figures, according to the author?

3. Woodward suggests that the starting point for developing a Rights-Based Poverty Line is to establish an agreed set of indicators reflecting economic and social rights such as what?

How we define poverty is critically important. Poverty is a moral concept: 'poor' is something we consider that people should not be. So, by setting our poverty targets according to a particular poverty line, we are saying that it is quite acceptable for people to live at that level of income, just as long as they don't fall below it.

The Dollar-a-Day Poverty Line

Millennium Development Goal One defines poverty as having an income below the dollar-a-day line—although actually this is now [2010] $1.25 per person per day, at purchasing power parity (PPP), at 2005 prices. This means that it is an income which would buy the same as $1.25 a day in the US in 2005.

This is extraordinarily low by any standards. Living on $1 (or indeed $1.25) per person per day in the US or any other developed country would be fairly unthinkable. A few years ago, I did some rough calculations to show what a dollar a day would mean in Britain. In 2006, it was equivalent to 35 people living on a single minimum wage, with no benefits of any kind, no gifts, borrowing, scavenging, begging or savings to draw on (since these are all included as 'income' in poverty calculations), and no free health services or education (since these are not generally available to the poor).

It is therefore not surprising that living conditions at this level of income are little short of appalling. Adam Wagstaff, a World Bank economist, estimated in 2003 that children living at (not below) the dollar-a-day line in a typical developing country had between a 1-in-12 and 1-in-6 chance of dying before their fifth birthday, compared with about 1-in-140 in developed countries. The great majority of these deaths are undoubtedly directly or indirectly poverty related; and between a third and half of those who survive are stunted by chronic malnutrition.

The Use of Purchasing Power Parity

It is difficult to argue that it is morally acceptable for people to live at this level of income, so long as they do not fall below it. But this is exactly what the Millennium Development Goals (MDGs) imply.

Clearly, the dollar-a-day line is too low; and it is too low because it is essentially arbitrary. There is nothing magical about an income of one dollar a day, and it certainly doesn't provide any assurance that people will be able to lead a decent life—or even survive beyond early childhood. It was originally picked as the average of the lowest 10 national poverty lines found in a survey of developing countries, even though these were themselves set in different—and in some cases equally arbitrary—ways. It has gone on being updated in essentially the same way. The problems with this approach go far beyond the level of the dollar-a-day line, to the whole way incomes are calculated in estimating poverty. So setting the line at $2, $3 or $4 a day instead, though perhaps more realistic, still wouldn't give us a meaningful measure of poverty.

The failure of the current system arises largely from the use of purchasing power parity (PPP)—or, to be more precise, from the way it is calculated. In theory, PPP exchange rates are based on comparing the prices of the same basket of goods and services in different countries. This is more sensible than using a market exchange rate, which would set the poverty line too high in countries with an undervalued exchange rate and too low where it is overvalued.

Clearly, the dollar-a-day line is too low; and it is too low because it is essentially arbitrary.

But the PPP exchange rates used are designed for comparing countries' national income, not people's poverty—so they reflect total spending in the country, public as well as private. Poor people, by definition, spend much less than rich people.

Even where they are a large majority of the population, they have only a small share of total spending. So PPP exchange rates overwhelmingly reflect the prices of goods and services bought by non-poor households, most of which are unaffordable by the poor anyway.

This is particularly problematic because the spending patterns of poor households differ systematically from those of the better off. The poor spend a large proportion—often a majority—of their incomes on basic staple foods, which account for a relatively small proportion of the spending of the better off, and therefore of the country as a whole. And the prices of basic foods vary far less between countries than other goods, and especially services, which are consumed more by the better off. The result is to set the poverty line at an artificially low level.

An Unreliable Approach

The seriousness of this can be demonstrated by the effects of the 2008 food crisis, when the prices of basic foods such as maize and rice—on which many poor households depend—more than doubled in a matter of months. For a poor household spending half its income on maize, the effect of doubling its price is disastrous. There is no money left for anything else. But if maize represents only, say, five per cent of total spending in the country, doubling its price will increase the poverty line by only five per cent. The poverty line should go up by 50 per cent, but is actually increased by only five per cent, concealing a very considerable rise in poverty.

By its nature, the dollar-a-day approach only takes account of incomes. But this is only one part of what makes poor people poor. To live on $1 a day with access to free or affordable health services and education, and reasonable living environments and working conditions, is bad enough. Without these advantages, it is considerably worse. But these are not reflected in poverty figures, wherever the threshold is set. The

UN [United Nations] Human Development Index and Human Poverty Index represent a creditable and worthwhile attempt to fill this gap; but they fall short of fully resolving the problem.

Every decade or so, PPP exchange rates are recalculated using a later base year. In principle, this should make no difference to estimates of poverty, but actually the effects can be dramatic.

By its nature, the dollar-a-day approach only takes account of incomes. But this is only one part of what makes poor people poor.

Using a base year of 1985, the proportion of people below the dollar-a-day line in Nigeria in 1993 was about the same as that in Mauritania. When the base year was updated to 1993, however, the poverty rate in Nigeria in the same year was 10 times what it was in Mauritania. The same updating increased the estimated level of poverty in sub-Saharan Africa by nearly half relative to that in Latin America. That a technical change which should make no difference makes such a big difference raises serious doubts about whether the dollar-a-day estimates are meaningful or reliable at all.

When the base year is updated, the poverty line is updated too—however, it is not updated in line with any measure of price inflation, but (somewhat arbitrarily) on the basis of national poverty lines. When the base year was updated from 1993 to 2005, the dollar-a-day line was reduced by 14 per cent in real terms, having already been reduced when the base year was updated from 1985 to 1993. But the estimated level of poverty at this lower poverty line was half as much again as had been estimated using the previous higher line.

If the poverty line had instead been adjusted for inflation, poverty in 1990—the starting point of the MDGs—would have been more than 49 per cent, nearly double the 28 per cent estimated before the 2008 update. Until two years ago, we thought the MDG was to halve poverty from 28 per cent. Now it seems, it is to reduce poverty to 24.5 per cent—only slightly below the point we thought we had started from.

A Better Approach

We need a new and better approach to defining and measuring poverty. First, we need to consider why we are concerned about poverty. It is not because people have less than $1 (or indeed $2, $3 or $10) a day—it is because they do not have enough income to allow them to live what we would consider a decent (or at least minimally adequate) life. So our aim should be to set the poverty line at a level where people can actually have a standard of living which we would consider morally acceptable.

Various alternative approaches have been proposed to deal with these problems—but none resolves them entirely. Either they rely on applying a single global poverty line using purchasing power parity, raising all the problems discussed above; or they depend on poor people spending their incomes on exactly the right things (and economists knowing what they are) and still only meeting their most basic need—an adequate calorie intake.

Our aim should be to set the poverty line at a level where people can actually have a standard of living which we would consider morally acceptable.

I have therefore proposed a new approach, which I have called the Rights-Based Poverty Line (RBPL). This moves away from the idea of setting a single global poverty line, to country-specific lines. But it also avoids the conventional approach of estimating country poverty lines according to the cost of a basket of goods and services considered to be essential. Instead, the aim is to set poverty lines in each country which correspond to the same level of outcome indicators, reflecting health, nutrition, education, access to water and sanitation, housing, and so on.

This enables us both to link the poverty line to actual living standards—without making artificial assumptions about what people will spend their income on—and to avoid the problem of exchange rates and purchasing power parity, while maintaining consistency between countries. The difference is that consistency will be based on what it means to live at a particular level of income, and not estimates of spending power in terms of goods poor people can't afford anyway.

Poverty is a complex phenomenon, and its nature varies considerably between different countries and communities.

The Need for a Set of Indicators

The starting point is to establish an agreed set of indicators which reflect economic and social rights—such as health, nutrition, education—and to set an agreed minimum level of each indicator that we consider to be morally acceptable. Based on the statistical relationship between income and each indicator in each country, we can then find the income at which the threshold minimum level is reached (on average)— and this is set as the poverty line corresponding with that indicator.

Of course, we need to decide which indicators to use, and what the threshold level should be for each. But, in a sense, this is part of the point of the exercise. Rather than allowing us to make an implicit moral judgment that a certain income is 'enough', without even considering what it means to live on that income, it makes us confront the question explicitly: Just how much do we consider to be 'enough'? How poor is 'too poor'?

This approach presents a more complex picture than the single headline numbers generated by the dollar-a-day system. In each country we have a number of different poverty lines, corresponding with the indicators we use; and for each line, we have two important indicators instead of one—the poverty line itself, and the proportion of the population below it. We also have two ways of reducing poverty. Either we can increase incomes, so that people move above the poverty line; or we can improve living standards at a given level of income, so that the poverty line itself is reduced.

The greater complexity of the RBPL approach can be seen as an advantage rather than a disadvantage. The simplicity of the dollar-a-day approach—its greatest triumph—is also a major limitation. Poverty is a complex phenomenon, and its nature varies considerably between different countries and communities. Any attempt to capture it in a single number will inevitably be an oversimplification. Neither can it provide us with a useful tool for policy making.

The Rights-Based Poverty Line

To tackle poverty effectively, we need an approach which will capture this complexity, but which we can make sense of, and relate to our reasons for wanting to reduce poverty.

The dollar-a-day approach can only tell us if income poverty is going up or down—and even that it cannot do reliably. The RBPL approach can give us a great deal of additional information on the relative importance of incomes compared with social provision and other factors, differentiating between different aspects of living standards—health, education, nutrition and so on. This, not how many people are below an arbitrary global poverty line, is the information needed for priority setting and decision making.

Don't get me wrong—none of this is intended as a criticism of the economists who originated and developed the dollar-a-day approach. Not only was this a very considerable intellectual and technical feat, but it has had a major political impact in putting poverty on the global agenda. When it was established 20 years ago, it was the best—indeed the only—tool we had for measuring poverty. Without it, there would never have been a Millennium Development Goal to halve poverty, and global poverty would no doubt have gone on being almost entirely ignored in international discussions.

But that was 20 years ago—and over this time, the weaknesses of the dollar-a-day approach have become increasingly apparent, without the approach having been improved to deal with them. It served the purpose of the time, by putting poverty on the agenda; but now that poverty is on the agenda, we need an approach which will give us a more reliable and detailed picture of poverty, so that we can make the right decisions to try to reduce it. The Rights-Based Poverty Line would be one way of doing this.

Periodical and Internet Sources Bibliography

The following articles have been selected to supplement the diverse views presented in this chapter.

Kaushik Barua	"Poverty Is About More than Money," *Guardian* (UK), August 4, 2010.
Alyssa Katharine Ritz Battistoni	"The Reality of Poverty," *Nation*, October 8, 2007.
Nate Berg	"Who's Poor? It Depends on Where You Live, Some Say," *Christian Science Monitor*, August 27, 2008.
Laurence Chandy and Geoffrey Gertz	"Missing Poverty's New Reality: There's a Lot Less of It," *Washington Post*, January 26, 2011.
Nicholas Eberstadt	"A Poverty of Statistics," *American*, September 18, 2010.
Economist	"A Wealth of Data: A Useful New Way to Capture the Many Aspects of Poverty," July 29, 2010.
Dan Morrell	"Who Is Poor?," *Harvard Magazine*, January/February 2011.
New York Times	"Counting the Poor," April 17, 2007.
Bill Steigerwald	"Are Our 37 Million Poor Really Poor?," *Human Events*, September 10, 2007.
Laura Wheaton and Jamyang Tashi	"Measuring Poverty," Urban Institute, February 15, 2010. www.urban.org.
World Bank and International Monetary Fund	"Global Monitoring Report 2010—The MDGs After the Crisis," 2010. http://web.worldbank.org.

CHAPTER 2

The Experience
of Poverty Around
the World

African Poverty Is Falling . . . Much Faster than You Think

Maxim Pinkovskiy and Xavier Sala-i-Martin

In the following viewpoint, Maxim Pinkovskiy and Xavier Sala-i-Martin argue that poverty reduction efforts in Africa have been more successful than people think. Pinkovskiy and Sala-i-Martin claim that their methodology for measuring poverty shows that between 1995 and 2006 African welfare improved dramatically. They conclude that Africa is on track to have half as much poverty as 1990 sometime before 2020. Arguing against other scholars, Pinkovskiy and Sala-i-Martin claim that their research shows that disadvantageous geography and troubled history have not been barriers to poverty reduction. Pinkovskiy is a graduate student in economics at the Massachusetts Institute of Technology and Sala-i-Martin is a professor of economics at Columbia University.

As you read, consider the following questions:

1. According to Pinkovskiy and Sala-i-Martin, African poverty declined by how much between 1990 and 2006?

2. The poor performance of what African country over the last decade is impeding the achievement of the Millennium Development Goals, according to the authors?

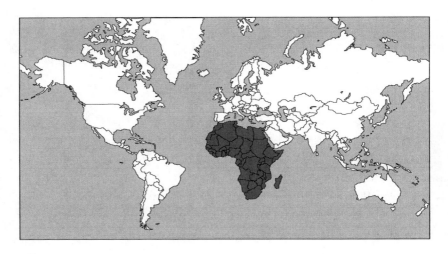

3. According to Pinkovskiy and Sala-i-Martin, have geographical and historical disadvantages in particular African countries been obstacles to reducing poverty?

*Sub-Saharan Africa has made little progress in reducing ex-
treme poverty, according to the latest Millennium Development Report. This column presents evidence from 1970 to 2006
to the contrary.*

The picture of Africa as a place of collapse, hunger, disease
and death is slowly fading. Both official statistics and the
popular press acknowledge a nascent "African Renaissance", as
the continent is enjoying its longest and strongest growth
spurt since independence.

Nevertheless, it is still widely believed that this growth is
primarily driven by oil and natural resource prices, and that it
is confined to well-connected elites in geographically advantaged countries. The popular image is that the poor majority
in all African nations and many African nations as a whole are
stuck in "poverty traps" created by unfortunate geography and
calamitous history. For example, the prospects of meeting the
first Millennium Development Goal of "halving, between 1990
and 2015, the proportion of people earning an income less

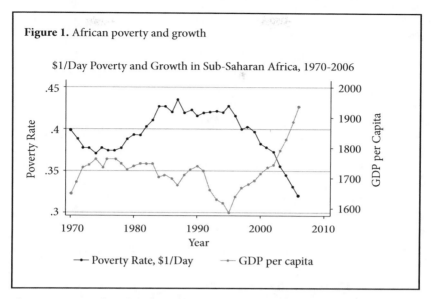

Figure 1. African poverty and growth

$1/Day Poverty and Growth in Sub-Saharan Africa, 1970-2006

than $1 a day" seem to appear bleak for Africa; the UN writes in its latest Millennium Development Report that *"little progress was made in reducing extreme poverty in sub-Saharan Africa"* (UNDP 2008).

We disagree. The sustained African growth of the last 15 years has engendered a steady decline in poverty that puts Africa on track to meet the goals by 2017. If peace is established in the Democratic Republic of the Congo, and it returns to the African trend (which is what happened to other African nations that were formerly at war), Africa will halve its $1/day income poverty rate by 2013, two years ahead of the 2015 target.

Moreover, African poverty reduction has been extremely general. Poverty fell for both landlocked and coastal countries, for mineral-rich and mineral-poor countries, for countries with favourable and unfavourable agriculture, for countries with different colonisers, and for countries with varying degrees of exposure to the African slave trade. The benefits of growth were so widely distributed that African inequality actually fell substantially.

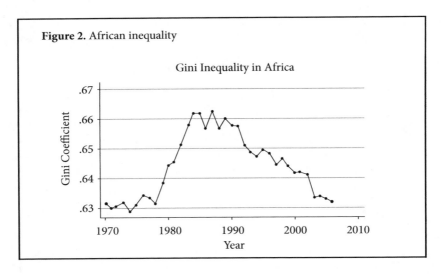

Figure 2. African inequality

Gini Inequality in Africa

Measuring African Poverty

In recent research (Pinkovskiy and Sala-i-Martin 2010), we use the methodology of our previous paper (Pinkovskiy and Sala-i-Martin 2009), to combine the standard Penn World Table GDP series with a comprehensive inequality database to estimate African income distribution for the period 1970–2006. For countries and years with inequality data, we compute the distribution of income by fitting a lognormal distribution to the inequality data, whereas for countries and years without inequality data, we interpolate inequality on the basis of neighbouring years. If a country has no inequality data for the sample period, we interpolate on the basis of the average inequality of countries with inequality data.

Figure 1 presents our main result:

- Using the $1/day definition of poverty adopted by the Millennium Development Goals, African poverty declined strikingly, from 41.6% in 1990 to 31.8% in 2006.[1]

1. Martin Ravallion (2010) argues that the poverty line should be defined using consumption rather than income, and that greater weight should be placed on poverty counts rather than poverty rates. However, we consider our definition of poverty is consistent with the one used by the Millennium Development Goals. See our response to Ravallion here [http://www.salaimartin.com/academics-and-books/65-altres/552-response-to-martin-ravallion-and-the-world-bank.html].

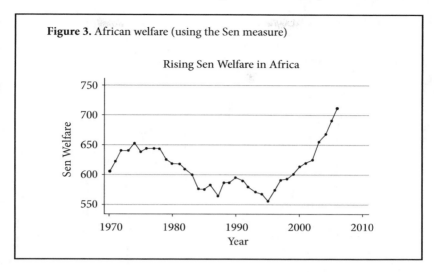

Figure 3. African welfare (using the Sen measure)

- Poverty seems to co-move with GDP almost perfectly.

- African inequality has also fallen over this period, almost entirely reversing its rise since 1970, but still remaining at a high absolute level (Figure 2).

Thus, during the period of positive and sustained African growth (1995 to 2006), not only did inequality not fail to explode as would have been the case if all the growth went to a narrow elite, but it actually declined substantially.

Our estimates of African inequality allow us to measure African welfare, e.g., by Amartya Sen's (1976) index of GDP-per-capita x1 minus the Gini coefficient. African welfare declined substantially between 1970 and 1995, but the trend was reversed dramatically between 1995 and 2006 (Figure 3). During this decade, however, the two components of the index moved in the same direction. Mean income increased and overall inequality declined. Hence, African welfare improved.

Implications for the Millennium Development Goals

Tables in our working paper show the expected decline in poverty by 2015 if present trends continue, and the expected

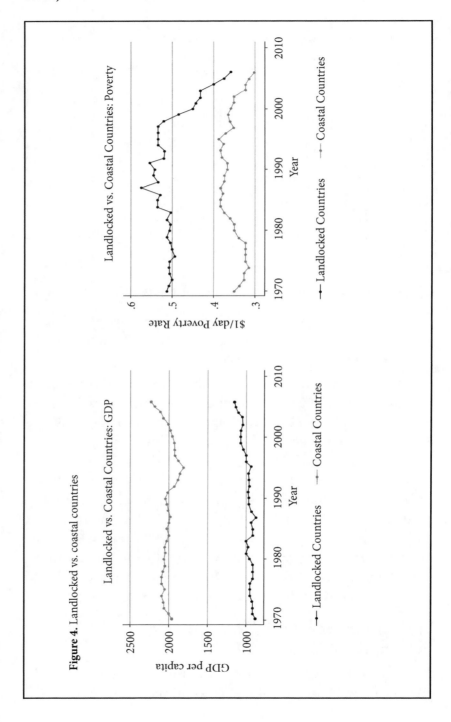

Figure 4. Landlocked vs. coastal countries

date of attainment of the goals for the baseline estimation method and multiple variations to the estimation procedure. We consider alternative methods of extrapolation, distributional assumptions other than the lognormal, an "adjusted" method of fitting distributions to the data that makes use only of data in the middle of the income distribution that should be less affected by survey misreporting, recovering the distribution by inverting the Gini coefficient, and using other sources of GDP besides the Penn World Tables. The data compiled by Angus Maddison and the World Bank's calculations of GDP after its revision of purchasing power parity estimates in 2007.

We also consider what happens if any of the eight largest African countries is dropped from the analysis. We see that Africa will probably halve poverty relative to 1990 sometime between 2015 and 2020, with the baseline estimate being 2017; a few years late relative to the Millennium Development Goal target. However, being a few years late to achieve the goal is much better than not making progress towards it at all. The main point is that Africa has been moving in the right direction and, while progress has not been as substantial and spectacular as in Asia, poverty has been falling and it has been falling substantially. We should not let the literal interpretation of the millennium goals turn good news (Africa is rapidly moving in the right direction) into bad news (Africa will not achieve the goals on time) (Easterly 2009).

One reason why the millennium goals are projected to be achieved several years late is the poor performance of the Democratic Republic of the Congo (DRC) over the last decade. Naturally, this poor economic performance has to do with the war that took place in that country during that decade, and which is now drawing to a close. If we exclude the DRC from our baseline computation, Africa halves poverty by 2012, three years ahead of time. (For more extensive robustness checks for the scenario without the DRC, see our paper;

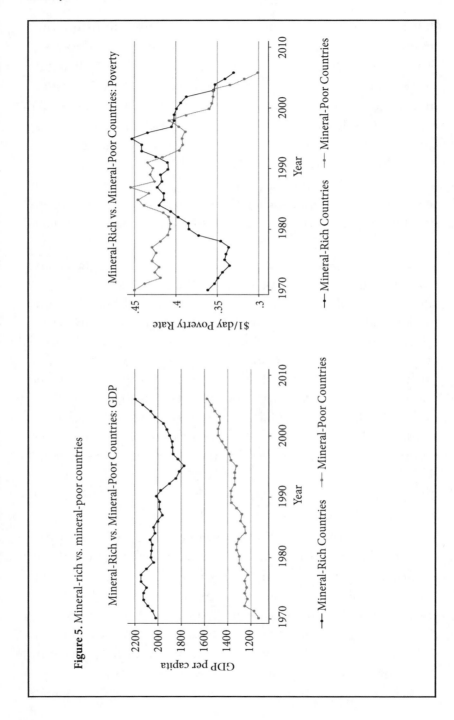

Figure 5. Mineral-rich vs. mineral-poor countries

these show that for most of nations, the MDG is actually achieved ahead of the 2015 target date.)

Why Africa Is Held Back

It has often been suggested that geography and history matter significantly for the ability of Third World, and especially African, countries to grow and reduce poverty. Collier (2006) argues that coastal countries, or countries that are mineral rich, will perform better than landlocked and mineral-poor countries in general. Bloom and Sachs (1998) point to adverse geography as a cause of slow development: In particular, countries that have unfavourable agriculture should be poorer than countries with more favourable conditions.

Others have suggested that troubled history may have a persistent effect on growth performance. Nunn (2007 and 2008), for example, argues that the African slave trade had *"particularly detrimental consequences, including social and ethnic fragmentation, political instability and a weakening of states, and the corruption of judicial institutions"* which led the parts of Africa most affected by the slave trade to grow much slower than the parts that were not. La Porta et al. (1999) suggest that the identity of the coloniser mattered substantially for development. Since these factors are permanent (and cannot be changed with good policy), they imply that some parts of Africa may be at a persistent growth disadvantage relative to others.

Yet Figures 4–9 show that the African poverty decline has taken place ubiquitously, in countries that were slighted as well as in those that were favoured by geography and history. For every breakdown discussed above, the left panel of the corresponding Figure shows GDP in countries to each side of the breakdown, while the right panel shows poverty rates. While the levels of the poverty series start out matching the hypotheses set out above, the poverty rates for countries on either side of the breakdown tend to converge, with the disad-

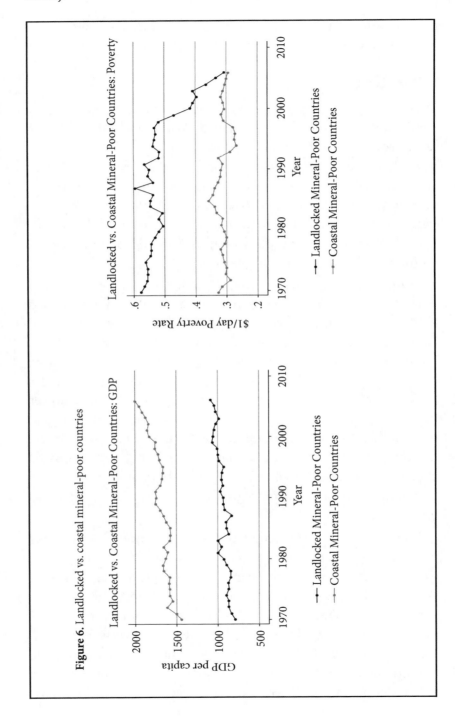

Figure 6. Landlocked vs. coastal mineral-poor countries

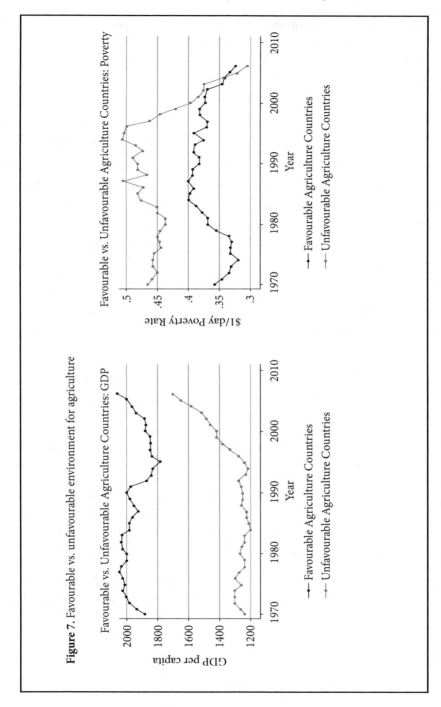

Figure 7. Favourable vs. unfavourable environment for agriculture

vantaged countries reducing poverty significantly to catch up to the advantaged ones. Neither geographical nor historical disadvantages seem to be insurmountable obstacles to poverty reduction.

Conclusions

Our main conclusion is that Africa is reducing poverty, and doing it much faster than many thought.

- The growth from the period 1995–2006, far from benefiting only the elites, has been sufficiently widely spread that both total African inequality and African within-country inequality actually declined over this period.

- The speed at which Africa has reduced poverty since 1995 puts it on track to achieve the Millennium Development Goal of halving poverty relative to 1990 by 2015 on time or, at worst, a couple of years late.

- If DRC converges to the African trend once it is stabilised, the MDG will be achieved by 2012, three years before the target date.

We also find that the African poverty reduction is remarkably general.

- African poverty reduction cannot be explained by a large country, or even by a single set of countries possessing some beneficial geographical or historical characteristic.

- All classes of countries, including those with disadvantageous geography and history, experience reductions in poverty.

This observation is particularly important because it shows that poor geography and history have not posed insurmountable obstacles to poverty reduction.

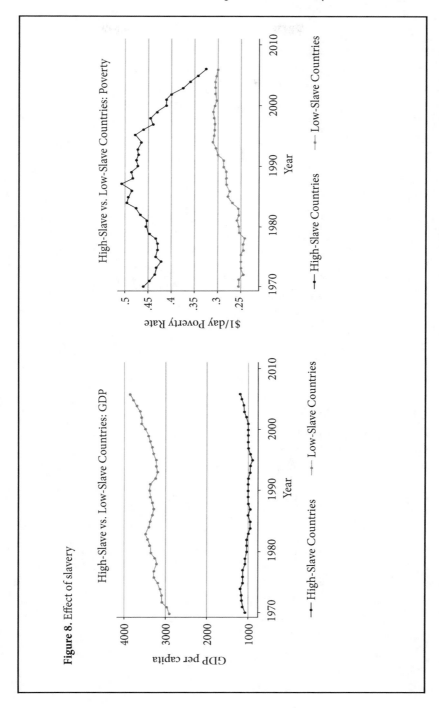

Figure 8. Effect of slavery

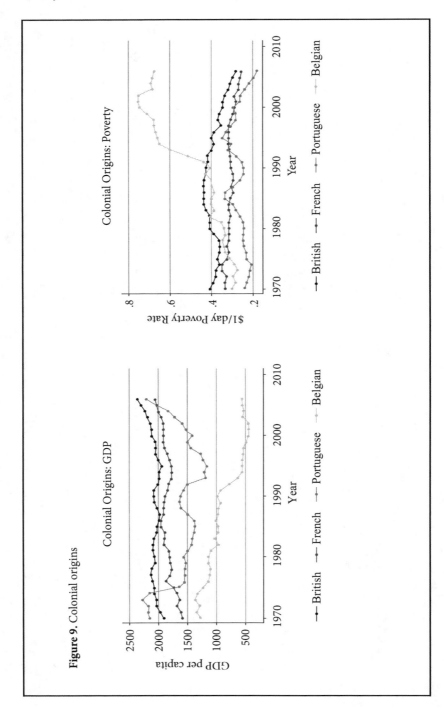

Figure 9. Colonial origins

The lesson we draw is largely optimistic—even the most blighted parts of the poorest continent can set themselves firmly on the trend of limiting and even eradicating poverty within the space of a decade.

References

Bloom, David E, and Jeffrey D Sachs (1998), "Geography, Demography, and Economic Growth in Africa", *Brookings Papers on Economic Activity*, 2:207-273.

Collier, Paul (2006), "Africa: Geography and Growth", *Journal TEN*, Federal Reserve Bank of Kansas City, Fall.

Easterly, William (2009), "How the Millennium Development Goals are Unfair to Africa", World Development, January.

The Economist (2010), "Uncaging the Lions", 10 June.

La Porta, Rafael, Florencio Lopez de Silanes, Andrei Shleifer and Robert Vishny (1999), "The Quality of Government", *Journal of Law, Economics and Organization*, 15(1):222-79.

Nunn, Nathan (2007), "The Historical Origins of Africa's Underdevelopment", VoxEU.org, 8 December.

Nunn, Nathan (2008), "The Long-Term Effects of Africa's Slave Trades", *Quarterly Journal of Economics*, 123(1):139-176.

Pinkovskiy, Maxim and Xavier Sala-i-Martin (2009), "Parametric Estimations of the World Distribution of Income", NBER Working Paper 15433.

Pinkovskiy, Maxim and Xavier Sala-i-Martin (2010), "African Poverty is Falling . . . Much Faster than You Think!", NBER Working Paper 15775.

Ravallion, Martin (2010), "Is African poverty falling?", Worldbank.org, 3 May.

United Nations (2008), *The Millennium Development Goals Report*.

World Bank (2004), "Millennium Development Goals".

South Asia Has the Largest Concentration of Poverty in the World

Ejaz Ghani

In the following viewpoint, Ejaz Ghani argues that there is a poverty problem in South Asia that is not being tackled properly. Ghani claims that the economic growth of the leading regions in South Asia has masked the widespread poverty of other regions. Ghani claims that economic growth can help these lagging regions but not until barriers to human mobility are removed and agricultural policies are revisited. Ghani is an economic advisor on South Asian poverty reduction and economic management at the World Bank and an editor of The Poor Half Billion in South Asia—What Is Holding Back Lagging Regions?

As you read, consider the following questions:

1. According to Ghani, the number of people living on less than $1.25 a day in South Asia increased by how many between 1981 and 2005?

2. The author identifies what four problems as South Asia's worst problems, which are concentrated in its lagging regions?

3. What two reasons does Ghani give in support of the view that regional development policies are not a solution?

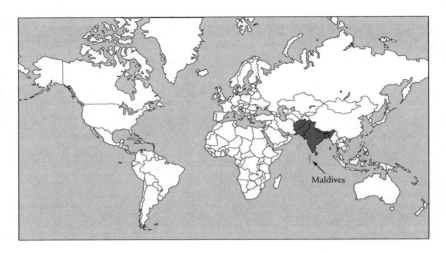

Maldives

outh Asia presents a depressing paradox. It is among the
Sfastest growing regions in the world, but it is also home to
the largest concentration of people living in debilitating poverty, conflict, and human misery. While South Asia is far more
developed than sub-Saharan Africa, and India (the largest
country in the region) has achieved lower middle-income status, South Asia has many more poor people than sub-Saharan
Africa.

The Two South Asias

This raises the big question of whether the best escape from
poverty comes from general economic *growth* or from a *direct
attack* on poverty. The answer depends on where one looks.
Stupendous growth hides deep pockets of poverty. For the
countries of South Asia, poverty has morphed from a national
to a sub-national problem.

Although economic growth has reduced South Asia's poverty rate, it has not fallen fast enough to reduce the total
number of poor people. The number of people living on less
than $1.25 a day increased from 549 million in 1981 to 595
million in 2005. In India, which accounts for almost three-
quarters of this population, the numbers increased from 420

million to 455 million during this period. Besides the slow pace of poverty reduction, human development has not kept up with the pace of income growth, either.

A lot of attention has been given to the "Shining Asia," while the "Suffering Asia" has been forgotten.

There are more than 250 million children in South Asia who are undernourished, and more than 30 million children who do not go to school. Over one-third of adult women are anemic. The share of female employment in total employment is among the lowest in the world.

Indeed, South Asia, with deeper regional disparities than the rest of the world, is really two South Asias. A lot of attention has been given to the "Shining Asia," while the "Suffering Asia" has been forgotten. The gap between them is so wide that they seem to be anchored in two different centuries. Worse still, it continues to increase.

The Impact of Growth

The leading regions have experienced rapid growth. They have acted as gateways connecting South Asia to the developed world, and have benefited from globalization, education, capital accumulation, and technological advancement. This is sustainable as there is . . . room for South Asia to catch up to rich countries' productivity levels.

This transformation has become a virtuous circle where initial growth has spiraled into greater growth, leading to more growth. Some leading regions in India are now the envy of other middle-income countries. Indeed growth can eliminate poverty in leading regions in a generation. But the lagging regions are doing no better than many sub-Saharan African countries. Indeed, their social and human development indicators are worse than in sub-Saharan Africa.

South Asia's worst problems—poverty, conflict, hunger, and gender inequalities—are largely concentrated in its lagging regions, where there are limits to growth, because geography, institutions, and globalization will continue to favor the concentration of economic activity in the leading regions. With migration to leading regions low, poverty remains concentrated in the lagging regions.

What can be done? There is no universal "fix" in economic development, and pluralism of approaches has great value. The challenge is to find what works best in which setting.

While economic growth is critical for poverty reduction, reviving growth in lagging regions will take time. Rather than wait for a rising tide to lift all boats, policy makers should consider *direct* policy interventions to reduce poverty. A direct attack on poverty can yield a double dividend: in reducing human misery, it could *spark* growth, thereby creating more political space for direct poverty reduction.

Interventions to Reduce Poverty

A high priority should be given to increasing pro-poor fiscal transfers. Lagging states spend considerably less than leading states on social services, including education and health care. Poor regions have a low base of economic activity to tax, which prevents them from investing in human and physical capital. Achieving equity through fiscal transfers can ensure a level playing field.

But simply directing financial resources to lagging regions will not be enough to solve their problems. For example, the gains from labor mobility have not been equally shared between educated and uneducated migrants. The gains are much higher for skilled workers, so the mobility rate increases with education. The mobility of university graduates is much higher than the mobility of unskilled workers.

Removing barriers to human mobility—such as labor laws, state-specific social-welfare programs, and housing-market

Rising Regional Inequality in South Asia

Despite recent growth and poverty reduction, South Asia still has nearly 400 million poor people (out of a population of 1.37 billion). Poverty is not just endemic, but increasingly concentrated in particular lagging regions. Not only are these regions poorer, but their growth rates are substantially slower than the better-off regions.

The phrase "two Indias" exemplifies this difference in regional development outcomes. In 2002–2003, all-India per capita GDP [gross domestic product] was $480; the poorest seven states (accounting for 55 percent of the population) had a per capita GDP that was two-thirds the national average, while in the richest seven states (33 percent of the population) per capita GDP was nearly double that of the poorest seven states. In the two largest and poorest northern states (Bihar and Uttar Pradesh, 25 percent of total population) per capita GDP was less than half the national average and only a third of the richest seven states. The four southern states, Andhra Pradesh, Karnataka, Kerala and Tamil Nadu (21 percent of the total population), at an average, enjoyed more than twice the GDP per capita of the quarter of the population concentrated in the two poorest northern states.

Shantayanan Devarajan and Ijaz Nabi,
"Economic Growth in South Asia: Promising,
Un-equalizing, . . . Sustainable?," World Bank, June 2006.

distortions—should be an integral part of development. Human mobility promotes growth and reduces poverty. It also empowers traditionally disadvantaged groups, particularly women.

Likewise, slow agricultural growth has constrained economic opportunities for the vast majority of poor people in lagging regions. Policy makers should recast agriculture in the new environment of globalization, supply chains, and growing domestic demand. The food-price crisis of two years ago served as a wake-up call, and has created an opportunity to revisit existing agricultural policies.

South Asia is at a critical stage in its historical transformation, when deepening economic disparities could stifle growth itself.

Regional development policies to promote so-called "equitable growth" are not a solution, for two reasons. First, empirical evidence shows that convergence of *per capita* income between lagging and leading regions is neither a necessary nor a sufficient condition for achieving poverty reduction and social convergence. Second, regional policies that promote "balanced" growth could lower overall growth, thereby impeding poverty reduction.

South Asia is at a critical stage in its historical transformation, when deepening economic disparities could stifle growth itself. If not addressed through direct measures, all of Asia will suffer.

China Has Made Great Strides in the Elimination of Poverty

M.K. Pandhe

In the following viewpoint, M.K. Pandhe argues that China has made much progress in the last three decades in eliminating poverty. Pandhe claims that government efforts to create jobs and provide education, health care, and social security have all helped to eliminate poverty. Pandhe contends that a current challenge for continued poverty eradication is the opposition to economic reform by ethnic minorities in the country. Although the global recession slowed down efforts to reduce poverty, Pandhe is confident that continued efforts will reduce poverty even further. Pandhe is a leader of the Communist Party of India and general secretary of the Centre of Indian Trade Unions (CITU).

As you read, consider the following questions:

1. According to Pandhe, how many people in China were facing poverty in 1978?

2. The author claims that absolute poverty in autonomous areas of minorities in China was how much higher than the country's average in 2007?

3. From 1986 to 1993, absolute poverty in China declined by an average of how many million people per year, according to Pandhe?

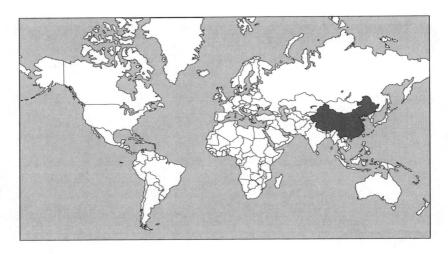

In the six decades of establishment of socialism, China has been trying to abolish poverty.

Progress in Poverty Reduction

There was some progress in the direction of reduction in poverty prior to the cultural revolution and remarkable improvement in the standard of living of the people had taken place. However, during the cultural revolution period, there were some problems. By the year 1978, there were 250 million people in China facing poverty levels.

Since 1978, the Chinese government adopted a policy of economic reforms which paid special attention to faster economic development and eradication of poverty. According to a statement by the state council of China in 2008, "In the past 50 years since the founding of New China especially since the initiation of reform and opening up to the outside world, the Chinese government has always put the people's right to subsistence and development first, focused on economic construction and made efforts to develop social productivity. Consequently, China's economy and society have advanced by leaps and bounds; its comprehensive national strength has been raised and the people's livelihood has improved by a huge margin thereby realizing two historic leaps bringing the people from poverty to having enough to eat and wear and then to living a better life."

During [the period between] 1980 and 2010 the per capita real standard of living of the entire population increased eight times, bringing a large section of the poverty-stricken people towards a decent living standard. In the year 1980, more than four billion yuan [$625 million] were allotted to poverty eradication programs. Thus from 1978 to 1986, the people below the poverty line came down from 250 million to 120 million.

In 1986, during the seventh five-year plan, poverty alleviation was given a top priority. People were given tax concession and other facilities. From 1986 to 1993 the impoverished people nationwide were reduced from 120 million to 80 million. Poverty was thus reduced by 6.4 million per year.

From 1978 to 1986, the people below the poverty line came down from 250 million to 120 million.

Sustained efforts to improve the standard of living of people and quality of life had a very important role to play in [the] poverty eradication program. More job creation was a crucial measure taken up by the government. In three decades since 1978, 37 crore (370 million) jobs were created by the government of China. Nine year compulsory education was introduced and in 2008 the rate of enrollment stood at 99.5 percent and junior middle schools reached 98.5 percent. Due to improved health care and social security measures the life expectancy increased since 1978 by five years to reach 73 years! [Since] 1978 infant mortality rate declined by 56 percent reaching 15.3 percent, while the maternity mortality rate dropped by 60 percent since 1978. All these measures had a positive impact on reducing overall poverty levels of the Chinese population.

Barriers to Poverty Elimination

One of the different problems China is facing today in the task of elimination of poverty is that a large part of the impoverished population belongs to ethnic minorities. They live in remote backward areas like Dingri, Gansu, Ningxia, Guangxi, Yunnan, Guizhou, Sichuan and Tibet. They were victims of centuries-old feudal exploitation, slavery, primitive society and serfdom. People from inner Mongolia also to some extent come in this category. In 2007, the incidence of people in absolute poverty in autonomous areas of minorities in China was 6.4 percent—4.8 percentage points higher than the country's average of 1.6 percent. Their number stood 77.4 lakhs (7.74 million) accounting for 52.3 percent of the country's total of one crore forty-seven lakhs and nine thousand poor people (10,709,000). However, available statistics show that in 2007, a total of 18.5 lakh (1.85 million) people came back to absolute poverty due to natural calamities. The government of China has prepared a special package to overcome the problem.

As the number of impoverished people is declining, the task is becoming more and more difficult, since it is concentrated in remote areas where developmental needs are more and more complex.

A section of the ethnic minorities oppose economic reform, which is also an obstacle in this task. In Tibet, every step taken by the government to reduce poverty is considered as a step towards destroying Tibetan culture by [the] Dalai Lama whose thinking practically means continuation of poverty and backwardness is preserving age-long Tibetan culture.

The government of China is taking steps to develop [a] road and railway network and airports to extricate Tibet from the poverty conditions. The Indian press, backed by US imperialist agencies, has been making stories that the economic developments in Tibet have security concerns for India.

China's Poverty Alleviation Programs

In Xinjiang, with 16 lakh 59 meters of area in 1978, there were 53.2 lakh (5.32 million) people living without enough food and clothing. However, due to huge spending by the Chinese government, by 2000 the problem of basic subsistence was solved satisfactorily. Social security benefits were also provided to the vast masses of the people.

Since 1994, the Chinese government increased investment in poverty alleviation programs, three times in comparison with the investments made between 1986 to 1993. As a result of this, the absolute poverty declined by an average of over 60 lakh (6 million) per year. During 2000–2003, the poverty was reduced by over 30 lakhs (3 million).

The global economic recession however slowed down the poverty alleviation program. However, at the end of 2008, the impoverished population in rural areas was reduced to four crore (40 million)! As the number of impoverished people is declining, the task is becoming more and more difficult, since it is concentrated in remote areas where developmental needs are more and more complex. Yet efforts are being made by the Chinese government to provide funds for poverty alleviation programs.

The Chinese 12th five-year plan which is under consideration of the government is likely to emphasize faster economic growth of less developed regions and give special emphasis on eradication of the vestiges of poverty prevailing in the country. The plan (2010–2015) will further reduce the extent of poverty in the country and will pave the way for accelerating the economic growth of the country.

Latin America Has Experienced a Decline in Poverty and Inequality

Alicia Bárcena

In the following viewpoint, Alicia Bárcena argues that poverty rates in Latin American countries have dropped substantially in the twenty-first century, and income equality has also improved in most countries in Latin America and the Caribbean. In addition, she contends that the global financial crisis has not created drastic negative effects. Bárcena claims that the improvements are due to both growth and government policies. She concludes that to make further improvements, Latin American countries need to focus on equality in development. Bárcena is the United Nations executive secretary of the Economic Commission for Latin America and the Caribbean (ECLAC).

As you read, consider the following questions:

1. According to Bárcena, what percentage of Latin American citizens were unable to satisfy basic nutritional and non-nutritional needs in 2008?

2. According to the author, spending on social programs, as a share of overall public spending, grew by how much from 1990 to 2008?

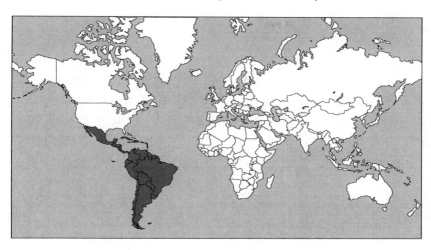

3. The author notes that at the center of the Economic Commission for Latin America and the Caribbean's (ECLAC's) comprehensive development strategy is what principle?

The years following the 2002 emerging market crisis have been good ones for Latin America. Economies grew smartly and there was a significant reduction in poverty and a slight improvement in income distribution—with only a small setback during the Great Recession that began in 2008. But even with these positive developments, poverty, inequality, and economic and social marginalization remain prevalent in many Latin American countries—which historically have had among the most skewed income distribution in the world.

A Reduction in Poverty

The improvements reflect not only strong economic growth in the region, which averaged more than 4 percent during the period, but also better social policies and an increase in the number of workers toiling in the formal economy rather than the less-productive underground, so-called informal, economy where wages and social protection are weaker.

Moreover, better monetary, spending, and tax policies—as well as strong demand for commodities key to the region's economies—enabled Latin American countries in the main to weather the global crisis better than advanced economies. In the past, worldwide downturns generally sent Latin American economies reeling—and poverty rates skyrocketing. This time the reduction in poverty recorded in the boom years before the crisis continued into 2010.

Despite sharp variation from country to country, poverty rates for the region as a whole dropped significantly between 2002 and 2008. On average, 44 percent of Latin American citizens were unable to satisfy basic nutritional and non-nutritional needs in 2002; by 2008 that number had fallen to 33 percent. Moreover, indigence—the level below which people cannot satisfy their food needs—also declined markedly, from about 19 percent in 2002 to less than 13 percent in 2008.

Despite sharp variation from country to country, poverty rates for the region as a whole dropped significantly between 2002 and 2008.

Improved Income Distribution

Like poverty, income inequality has also declined in most countries in Latin America and the Caribbean during the early years of the 21st century. If the so-called Gini coefficient is used to measure how equally incomes are distributed, 15 out of 18 economies surveyed in the region—Argentina, Bolivia, Brazil, Chile, Colombia, Ecuador, El Salvador, Honduras, Mexico, Nicaragua, Panama, Paraguay, Peru, Uruguay, and Venezuela—experienced improved income distribution. In at least 11 of these economies the improvement was larger than 5 percentage points. Only in Costa Rica, the Dominican Republic, and Guatemala did wealthier segments of society increase their share of total income. The Gini coefficient ranges between zero and 1. In an economy in which one person has all the income, the coefficient is 1. It is zero when everyone has the same income.

But income distribution in the region remains heavily skewed. The average per capita income of households in the upper 10 percent is about 17 times that of the poorest 40 percent, a slight improvement over 2002, when it was 20 times higher. So a number of households may have escaped poverty, but they are not benefiting much from economic growth. That should come as no surprise. Poverty, although endemic, responds much more to economic cycles than income distribution. Lack of income equity is a long-standing condition that reflects serious problems of social stratification and wealth inequality that have been handed down from generation to generation.

The improvements in poverty and income distribution are explained in large part by growth and government policies and the interaction between them. Many economies in the region have made significant efforts to increase the resources available to implement social policies. On average, social spending rose from 12.2 percent of gross domestic product (GDP) during 1990–91 to 18 percent of GDP during 2007–08. As a share of overall public spending, social programs grew from 45 percent to 65 percent.

Among key social policies, conditional transfer programs, which pay households that engage in socially useful behavior such as keeping children in school, have also helped improve income distribution and reduce poverty. Other important programs include unemployment insurance, recruitment subsidies, and job creation programs.

The Global Financial Crisis

Latin America was largely untouched by the first phase of the global crisis, which severely roiled financial markets in Europe and the United States. But the financial crisis spread to the

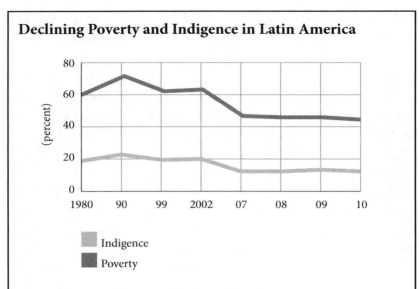

Declining Poverty and Indigence in Latin America

(percent)

1980 90 99 2002 07 08 09 10

■ Indigence
■ Poverty

TAKEN FROM: Alicia Bárcena, "Spreading the Wealth: Poverty and Inequality Have Declined in Latin America in Recent Years, but There Is a Lot More to Do," *Finance & Development*, March 2001.

real economy—which produces goods and services—and world trade shriveled in late 2008 and early 2009. Latin American output, as measured by GDP, fell 1.9 percent in 2009—the biggest annual contraction in two decades. But unlike during previous crises, many governments were able to undertake policies to mitigate the effects of the downturn on their citizens. Social policies became part of the effort—along with countercyclical taxing, spending, and monetary policies—that governments in the region took to soften the negative economic and social effects of the global crisis.

The generalized recovery in 2010 for most Latin American and Caribbean countries—led to a great extent by the adoption of countercyclical policies combined with improving conditions in the global economy—is expected to improve social conditions further. According to the latest estimates by the Economic Commission for Latin America and the Caribbean

(ECLAC), the region's poverty rate rose a tiny bit (from 33 percent to 33.1 percent) in 2009 and is expected to have declined a full percentage point in 2010, to 32.1 percent. Extreme poverty, which rose 0.4 percentage point in 2009, is expected to have fallen back to its 2008 level of 12.9 percent.

In addition to economic growth and better social policies, changes in labor markets helped reduce poverty and income inequality. In many countries jobs in the formal sector increased, which, together with rising hourly wages, helped lower-income households relatively more than better-off households.

Latin America was largely untouched by the first phase of the global crisis, which severely roiled financial markets in Europe and the United States.

Structural Constraints on Future Improvements

As encouraging as the improvements were, structural constraints could significantly hamper future improvements in overall economic welfare.

- Despite the recent movement of some workers from the informal to the formal sector, informal employment remains prevalent. Informal jobs, by their nature, are designed to remain out of sight and are seldom as productive as jobs in the formal sector. The productivity gap between the formal and informal sectors leads to wage differentials and inequality. Moreover, because informal employers often do not pay social security taxes, their workers usually are not as well protected as workers in the formal sector, leaving many people with inadequate health insurance and old-age protection.

- The unequal distribution of financial assets and real assets means that much of Latin American society is poorly equipped to weather economic and social instability.

- Less access to health and education by poorer people makes it harder to even out income distribution.

All these problems contribute to the region's continued structural productivity gaps—both within countries and compared with the rest of the world. That pervasive lagging productivity translates into low-paying employment and transmits poverty and inequality from generation to generation in a vicious cycle that is hard to break.

To deal with these structural issues, ECLAC has proposed a comprehensive development strategy to eradicate poverty and inequality. It places equality at the center of development. It establishes a vital role for government and calls for public-private partnership in the setting of economic and social policies.

ECLAC identifies three interlinked policies in its approach to production: industrial policy that focuses on the most innovative sectors, technology policy that increases and disseminates know-how, and policies to support small- and medium-sized enterprises.

Social equality and economic growth are not necessarily at odds: The great challenge is to find ways they can reinforce each other.

Employment, social, and education policies are at the core of the equality agenda. Labor policy alone does not generate employment, but it can help countries adapt to new conditions in the global market with fiscally and socially responsible economic protection for workers.

Social equality and economic growth are not necessarily at odds: The great challenge is to find ways they can reinforce each other.

Poverty in the Middle East and North Africa Varies Widely

Farrukh Iqbal and Mustapha Kamel Nabli

In the following viewpoint, Farrukh Iqbal and Mustapha Kamel Nabli argue that despite the image of the Middle East and North Africa as wealthy due to oil revenues, many areas of the region have extensive poverty. Iqbal and Nabli claim that the region has made progress in improving health and education, but this has not translated into better economic conditions for the poor. The authors conclude that the region needs economic growth, higher quality education, and equality of opportunity in order to address the existing poverty. Iqbal is the manager of the poverty reduction and economic management group in the Middle East and North Africa region of the World Bank. Nabli is the governor of Tunisia's central bank and former chief economist at the World Bank.

As you read, consider the following questions:

1. According to Iqbal and Nabli, what seven countries in the Middle East and North Africa (MENA) region do not collect systematic data on incomes and expenditures of their citizens?

2. The poverty rate in rural Upper Egypt is how many times larger than the rate in big cities, according to the authors?

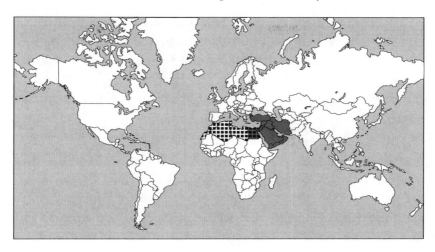

3. Unemployment rates in the MENA region average what, according to Iqbal and Nabli?

The current high price of oil is likely to reinforce a misleading image of the Middle East and North Africa (MENA) region, namely, that it is a rich region that uniformly provides a wide array of subsidized consumption goods and free social services to its citizens financed by revenues from plentiful supplies of oil and gas. For some countries in the region, especially the small oil states of the Gulf, this is an accurate image. For others, however, the image is misleading. With or without hydrocarbon resources, many countries in the region face significant challenges in fighting poverty and deprivation.

Data About Poverty

While poverty is not only about command over monetary resources, a monetary measure is a good place to start. To estimate poverty, the general practice is to collect information about income and spending through household surveys. When we review the data available to the World Bank, what do we find? To begin with, we find that several countries in the MENA region do not collect poverty data at all or, if they collect such data, they do not make the results public. In these countries there is no way of calculating how many people lack sufficient incomes to meet basic food and other expenditure needs. The number of such people may be high or low but the point is that it is not calculated, or if calculated, not reported.

But at least seven countries in the region do collect systematic data on the distribution of incomes or expenditures among their citizens and allow the World Bank access to aggregated versions of the results. These countries include Algeria, Egypt, Iran, Jordan, Morocco, Tunisia and Yemen. A recent World Bank review of country-level household survey data shows that there is much nuance and diversity to poverty patterns and trends in the region.

The available data show that, in recent years, about one in every five persons in the region could be considered poor at the $2 PPP line (PPP or purchasing power parity measures the amount of local currency that is needed to purchase the basket of goods and services that would cost $1 in the US). Furthermore, this proportion stayed roughly constant for most of the 1990s, fluctuating between 20 and 25 percent of the population. This stagnation in poverty rates mirrors the stagnation in regional economies over this period and highlights the importance of growth-promoting policies for the region.

> *The available data show that, in recent years, about one in every five persons in the region could be considered poor.*

Diversity in Poverty Rates

But the data also show considerable diversity among countries. For example, Egypt and Yemen feature poverty rates that are more than twice as high as the average for the region, reflecting conditions that are far removed from those of welfare states living comfortably off natural resources. On the other hand, Algeria, Jordan, Iran, Morocco and Tunisia feature rates that are bunched between 5 percent and 15 percent. And while the poverty trend in Egypt, Jordan and Morocco has fluctuated during the last decade, in Iran and Tunisia it has shown a fairly steady decline. A broadly similar pattern is found even when poverty rates are estimated using national minimum consumption standards.

While high oil prices are a boon for some countries, they could bring hard times for large net importers of oil.

National poverty lines reveal considerable diversity in poverty rates *within* countries as well. In most countries, some regions, provinces or governorates have much higher poverty rates than others. To take only one example, the poverty rate in rural Upper Egypt is almost seven times as high as that in the big cities or metropolitan areas. Substantial intra-country variations are common and indicate that the fruits of past growth and public spending have not been equally shared. Clearly, issues of inclusion and equal opportunity continue to be a challenge for MENA.

Will the oil-price boom that has prevailed for the last few years carry the region out of poverty? This depends on several considerations. Not all the countries in the region have large hydrocarbon resources. While high oil prices are a boon for some countries, they could bring hard times for large net importers of oil. In these countries, high oil prices increase production costs for businesses and generate fiscal pressures on governments. However, some countries can also benefit from flows of migration and remittances that exist within the region. For example, Egypt, Jordan and Yemen have historically benefited from such links with the oil-exporting countries of the Gulf. Will history repeat itself? So far, the evidence sug-

Poverty in MENA

The poverty rate in MENA [the Middle East and North Africa] has been declining over the period 1990–2005. The number of people in poverty, however, has not declined since 1990 due to rapid population growth, and by 2005 remained around 50 mln. [million] (under $2 a day). . . . As many as 17 percent of Egyptians, 15 percent of Yemenis and 10 percent of Moroccans have consumption levels which are no more than 50 cents per day above the international line of $2 a day, suggesting high vulnerability to economic shocks.

World Bank,
"Poverty in MENA," Sector Brief, 2008.

gests that the present oil boom is not producing regional spill-over effects that are as strong as those witnessed in the previous oil boom of the 1970s and early 1980s.

While it is appropriate to remain concerned about the challenge of income poverty, mention should also be made of experience with non-monetary aspects. Here the region has made tremendous progress. For example, between 1985 and 2000, literacy spread to 69 percent of the population from an initial level of 47 percent, average years of schooling (for those above 15) rose from 3.4 years to 5.2 years, the mortality rate for children under five years of age fell dramatically from 108 per thousand live births to only 46 per thousand and life expectancy rose from 61 years to 68 years. Indeed, by the year 2000, the MENA region had caught up with middle-income countries in many conventional human development indicators.

Economic Growth and Education

This remarkable result begs a question. Why was MENA's economic performance so poor in the last two decades or so despite rising levels of health and education? At least two interrelated possibilities can be considered for the case of education. First, rising education levels may have contributed positively to the economic performance of the MENA region but the impact may have been overshadowed by the negative effects of other factors such as the decline of public resources (and related infrastructure spending) due to weak prices for hydrocarbons and debt burdens carried over from a more profligate past, poor macroeconomic management, and lack of movement on key structural reforms such as opening the economy to the private sector and to international trade. Second, the returns on human capital may be low in MENA because of deficiencies in the quality and relevance of education. Or returns to education may be low because of the lack of integration with world markets. Both these possibilities are consistent with available data on rates of return and unemployment. The MENA region exhibits low rates of return to education, ranging from 2.5 percent to 10 percent for different levels. The region also has high rates of unemployment, averaging about 13 percent, but even higher among the educated and the young.

Looking to the future, we may emphasize three considerations. First, as already mentioned, the region needs higher and sustainable growth. If growth comes from a broad economic base and is sustained at around 3 percent per capita per annum, the poverty situation will improve dramatically over the next ten years. Calculations done by World Bank staff suggest that, in such a scenario, the poverty rate for the region could decline to 7 percent, or almost 13 percentage points lower than recently recorded levels.

Second, something must be done to improve the returns to education. The most promising option is to shift the focus of education policy from quantity to quality. Many MENA countries, though not all, have successfully met the initial challenge of putting children in school. Now the emphasis must shift to making sure that schools provide higher quality learning. As MENA economies move towards producing more for world markets, they will need to compete with other countries to secure larger market shares in both goods and foreign investment. The more skilled their workforces, the better equipped they will be to compete internationally. A shift towards better quality will help strengthen the education-income link in the region.

Most MENA countries have taken big strides towards equalizing opportunities through providing better health and education to their citizens.

Finally, we must look at the larger picture concerning equality of opportunity. Economic, political and social inequalities tend to trap disadvantaged people at the bottom of society for generation after generation. This is not only unfortunate for those at the bottom; it is also an impediment to higher economic growth over the long run. When those with ability are denied the opportunity to contribute fully to the economy, the economy suffers. Most MENA countries have taken big strides towards equalizing opportunities through providing better health and education to their citizens. But opportunities do not flow from better education and health services alone. They are affected as well by the scope for political voice, by a leveling of the political playing field together with the economic playing field. Here the countries of the region have a long road to travel.

Poverty in the United States Is Greater than in Other High-Income Countries

Timothy Smeeding

In the following viewpoint, Timothy Smeeding argues that the United States has more extensive poverty than most comparable countries, using both a relative poverty measurement and an absolute one. Smeeding also claims that the United States spends the least amount of its resources on antipoverty income transfer programs than similarly wealthy countries. Poor families with children, Smeeding says, are particularly worse off in America. By comparing the United States with the United Kingdom, Smeeding concludes that America needs to combine incentives to work with increased benefits in order to reduce poverty. Smeeding is a professor of economics and public administration at Syracuse University, where he also is director for the Center for Policy Research.

As you read, consider the following questions:

1. According to Smeeding, the US poverty line for a family of four, expressed as a percentage of median family income for four, has fallen by how much between 1960 and 2000?

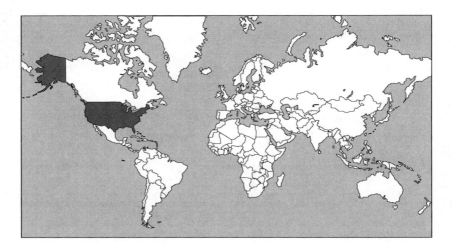

2. The United States spends half as much (as a share of gross domestic product) on antipoverty income transfer programs compared to which three countries, according to Smeeding?

3. According to the author, the relative child poverty rate in the United States is how many times greater in comparison to other rich countries?

Very few nations have an "official" measure of poverty. Only the United States and the United Kingdom have regular "official" poverty series. Statistics Canada publishes the number of households with incomes below a series of "low-income cutoffs" on a regular basis; Australia does so irregularly. But northern European and Scandinavian nations do not calculate official rates of poverty or low income. In these countries, the debate instead centers on the level of income at which minimum benefits for social programs should be set and on the issue of "social exclusion."

Relative and Absolute Poverty

Poverty can be measured either in relative terms, usually as compared to median income, or in absolute terms, as compared to purchasing a bundle of goods deemed to be the basic necessities in a given country. The United States, for example, relies on an "absolute" measure of poverty defined in the early 1960s by a government statistician, Mollie Orshansky, and held constant in real terms since that time.

In international comparisons, poverty must generally be treated as a relative concept, because in looking at poverty across nations with different levels of per capita GDP [gross domestic product], an absolute poverty standard will tend to produce either extremely high poverty rates in some countries or extremely low rates in other countries—or both. A majority of cross-national studies define the poverty threshold as one-half of national median income, and we will follow that convention in most of this [viewpoint]. For comparison, the official United States poverty line was just about 27 percent of median United States family pretax cash income in 2000 and about 32 percent of median United States disposable posttax household income. Alternatively, the United Kingdom and the European Union have selected a poverty rate of 60 percent of the median income. The pattern of the results we present using 50 percent of the median poverty standard is largely the same at a 40 percent level. However, the differences in poverty rates between the United States and other nations are much larger at the 60 percent of median line, which is about twice the United States poverty line, expressed as a percentage of national median income.

When poverty is defined in absolute terms, the World Bank and the United Nations Millennium Development movement define poverty in Africa and Latin America using an income threshold of $1 or $2 per person per day, and in central and eastern Europe a threshold of $2 or $3 per day. In contrast, the U.S. poverty line in absolute terms is six to twelve times higher than these standards. The U.S. poverty line for a family of four has in fact fallen from 48 to 29 percent of median census family income for four between 1960 and 2000. To address the absolute poverty issue in U.S. terms, we use both the official U.S. poverty line and 125 percent of this line to compare our estimates with the poverty estimates employed by others. We also calculate progress against absolute poverty across nations by "anchoring" poverty rates in the mid-1980s and comparing incomes for later years against this standard updated only by domestic price changes. . . .

Poverty can be measured either in relative terms, usually as compared to median income, or in absolute terms, as compared to purchasing a bundle of goods deemed to be the basic necessities in a given country.

Poverty in the United States, Canada and Europe

The relative poverty rate for all persons varies from 5.4 percent in Finland to 17.0 percent in the United States, with an average rate of 10.3 percent across the eleven countries. Higher poverty rates are found in Anglo-Saxon nations with a relatively high level of overall inequality, like the United States, Canada, Ireland and the United Kingdom; in Italy, with its wide north-south regional differential in income; and in geographically large and diverse countries, like the United States and Canada. Still, Canadian and British poverty are both about 12 percent and are, therefore, far below the U.S. levels. The lowest poverty rates are more common in smaller, well-developed and high-spending welfare states like Sweden and Finland, where they are about 5 or 6 percent. Middle-level rates are found in major European countries where unemployment compensation is more generous, where social policies provide more generous support to single mothers and working women (through paid family leave, for example) and where social assistance minimums are high. For instance, the Netherlands, Austria, Belgium and Germany have poverty rates that are in the 7 to 8 percent range.

On average, child poverty is a lesser problem than is elder poverty in these nations. But single parents and their children and elders generally have the highest poverty rates, while those in two-parent units, mixed units and the childless experience the least poverty. In general, elder poverty rates are somewhere between single parents, who are less well-off, and two-parent units, which are better-off, but this is not universally the case.

The United States has the highest or second highest relative poverty rate in each category except for childless adults, where our 11.2 percent rate is third. Poverty rates in the United States for persons living with children are nearly double the average rate. In most cases, Ireland has the highest or second highest poverty rate measured on a relative basis.

The United States has the highest or second highest relative poverty rate in each category except for childless adults, where our 11.2 percent rate is third.

Relative poverty rates are often taken as a proxy for inequality, since a more spread-out income distribution will tend to have a larger share of the population that has less than half of median income. Here, we take the income thresholds that determine the U.S. poverty and near-poverty rates for each different household size and then use PPP [purchasing power parity] exchange rates to convert them to poverty thresholds for nine countries. In this comparison, we exclude Italy and Ireland, because the ratio of disposable cash income to GDP is far below the levels in other countries, which suggests that income underreporting in the data is significantly different in these countries. Because the U.S. poverty line is such a low fraction of median disposable income—about 32 percent when household disposable income is used as the basis for comparison—we also use 125 percent of the U.S. poverty line to come closer to the standards used in other nations.

Using the official poverty line, the United States falls to second in the poverty ratings, with the United Kingdom having higher overall poverty rates using this standard. At the 125 percent line, the United States ranks fourth among these nations. The United States looks somewhat better using either of these "absolute" measures than with the relative measure due to its higher overall standard of living, a general finding that has been confirmed in other studies. In terms of vulnerable groups, however, poverty for U.S. children remains very high (ranking second by either standard) even within this set of rich nations. And poor U.S. residents, especially poor children, do not compare well to those in other nations based on PPP-adjusted real incomes. . . .

The Antipoverty Effect of Taxes and Transfers

In every nation, benefits from governments, net of taxes, reduce relative income poverty. . . . Remarkably enough, the U.S. relative poverty rate *before* taxes and transfers is actually below average for these countries, even though the United States ranks the highest of all the countries in this comparison group in relative poverty rates after taxes and transfers.

Given this divergence, it should be no surprise that, of the countries listed, the United States devotes by far the smallest share of its resources to antipoverty income transfer programs. In 2000, the United States spent less than 3 percent of GDP on cash and near-cash assistance for the nonelderly (families with children and the disabled). This amount is less than half the share of GDP spent for this purpose by Canada, Ireland or the United Kingdom; less than a third of spending in Austria, Germany, the Netherlands or Belgium; and less than a quarter of the amount spent in Finland or Sweden. These differences are primarily long term and secular, not related to the business cycle. Given this low level of cash antipoverty spending, similar calculations for absolute poverty would show roughly the same effects.

We split the antipoverty effect into two components: social insurance and taxes, and social assistance, and we do not take account of behavioral responses to antipoverty programs that might affect market incomes. The former type of benefit is not income- or means-tested and includes universal benefits such as child allowances and child tax credits; the latter is targeted to the otherwise poor using income tests. Most nations use both types of instruments. . . . The United States makes the least antipoverty effort of any nation, reducing relative poverty created by market incomes by 28 percent compared to the average reduction of 61 percent. The nations closest to the United States in terms of overall effect are Ireland and Canada. Most nations get at least a 50 percent poverty reduction from social insurance, and in heavily insured countries like Austria, Belgium and Germany, social insurance reduces poverty by 62 to 75 percent. In the case of social assistance, large effects of targeted programs are evident in Finland (34 percent) and the United Kingdom (33 percent reductions) and lower ones (under 10 percent) in the more socially insured nations like Austria, Germany, Belgium, the Netherlands and Canada. Detailed analysis confirms that higher levels of government spending as in Scandinavia and northern Europe and more careful targeting of government transfers on the poor as in Canada, Sweden and Finland produce lower poverty rates.

The United States devotes by far the smallest share of its resources to antipoverty income transfer programs.

The Working Poor and Child Poverty

The overall poverty figures can be sliced along many different dimensions: by gender, age, retirement status, ethnicity, immigration and others. For example, great strides have been made in reducing poverty among the elderly in most high-income countries over the past 40 years. Indeed, poverty among younger pensioners is no longer a major problem. However, poverty in older old age is almost exclusively an older women's problem. Three-quarters of the poor elders, age 75 or older, in each high-income nation are women; almost 60 percent of all poor age 75 and over in each nation are older women living alone. In the United States, the means-tested programs for the poor that are categorized in this [viewpoint] as "social assistance"—especially Supplemental Security Income (SSI) and food stamps—have almost no effect on altering the poverty rate among the elderly, because their combined benefit levels are set so low.

Comparative cross-national poverty rankings suggest that U.S. poverty rates are at or near the top of the range when compared with poverty rates in other rich countries.

However, here we will concentrate on one of the areas where poverty in the United States differs most greatly from the other comparison nations: the experience of poor families with children. In the United States, fewer than two million families with children are still on welfare, but there are 14.3 million families with children who have at least one worker, but are poor by the official poverty definition. . . .

A combination of labor market conditions and government programs affects poverty rates. . . . On average, lone-parent poverty rates are about three-and-a-half times larger than two-parent rates using either market income or disposable cash income. Social insurance and social assistance, on average, reduce poverty by another 23 percent each for single parents, and a slightly smaller amount for two-parent units. . . .

A Tale of Two Countries

Comparative cross-national poverty rankings suggest that U.S. poverty rates are at or near the top of the range when compared with poverty rates in other rich countries. The U.S. child and elderly poverty rates seem particularly troublesome. America's elders also have poverty rates that are high, particularly on relative grounds. In most rich countries, the relative child poverty rate is 10 percent or less; in the United States, it is 21.9 percent. What seems most distinctive about the American poor, especially poor American single parents, is that they work more hours than do the resident parents of other nations while also receiving less in transfer benefits than in other countries.

While acknowledging that the United States has greater poverty than other industrialized nations, some defenders of American economic and political institutions have argued that inequality plays a crucial role in creating incentives for people to improve their situations through saving, hard work and investment in education and training. In the long run, this argument goes, those with relatively low incomes might enjoy higher absolute incomes in a society where wide income disparities are tolerated than in one where law and social convention keep income differentials small. Indeed, in recent years, the relatively unequal United Kingdom and especially the U.S. economies have, in fact, performed better than other economies where income disparities are smaller. Employment growth (even since 2001) has been relatively faster, joblessness lower and economic growth higher in these countries than in many other OECD [Organisation for Economic Co-operation and Development] countries where public policy and social convention have kept income disparities low.

However, evidence that lower social spending in the United States and the United Kingdom "caused" higher rates of growth is not found in the literature. Moreover, while the real incomes of families with children did rise in the latter 1990s, most of the gains have been captured by Americans much further up the income scale. In 2000, the United States and the United Kingdom were the two nations in our comparison group with the highest rates of child poverty, although child poverty rates in both countries did decline in the mid to late 1990s owing mainly to the strong wage growth and tight labor markets in both countries.

The relationship between antipoverty spending and reductions in poverty is complex.

However, the United Kingdom made a substantial push toward reducing child poverty since 1999. In 2000–2001, the child poverty rate in the United States as measured by the U.S. Census Bureau was 15 percent. If that absolute poverty rate is converted and applied to the United Kingdom, the child poverty rate in the United Kingdom was also 15 percent in that year. Both the United States and United Kingdom economies hit a sour patch in the early 2000s. However, Britain has spent an *extra* 0.9 percent of GDP for low-income families with children since 1999. Nine-tenths of a percent of United States GDP is about $100 billion, which is more than the U.S. government now spends on the Earned Income Tax Credit, food stamps and TANF [Temporary Assistance for Needy Families] combined. The result of this spending in Britain is that the poverty rate for United Kingdom children had fallen to 11 percent by 2003–2004, while the official U.S. child poverty rate was at 18 percent in 2004 according to the U.S. Census Bureau. It seems unlikely that the U.S. labor market by itself will generate large reductions in poverty for families with children. Single parents with young children and those with low skills will all face significant challenges earning an income that lifts them out of poverty, no matter how many hours they work.

Of course, the relationship between antipoverty spending and reductions in poverty is complex. No one kind of program or set of programs are conspicuously successful in all countries. Social insurance, universal benefits (such as child allowances) and social assistance transfer programs targeted on low-income populations are mixed in different ways in different countries, as are minimum wages, other labor market regulations, worker preparation and training programs, work-related benefits (such as child care and family leave) and other social benefits. If the United States is to reduce poverty substantially, it will need to do a better job of combining incentives to work with an increase in benefits targeted to low-wage workers in low-income families. There is already evidence that such programs produce better outcomes for kids.

Periodical and Internet Sources Bibliography

The following articles have been selected to supplement the diverse views presented in this chapter.

Carmen DeNavas-Walt, Bernadette D. Proctor, and Jessica C. Smith — "Income, Poverty, and Health Insurance Coverage in the United States: 2010," US Census Bureau, September 2011. www.census.gov.

Eurostat — "Combating Poverty and Social Exclusion: A Statistical Portrait of the European Union, 2010," Publications Office of the European Union, 2010. http://epp.eurostat.ec.europa.eu.

Kristin Fryer — "Poverty in Canada," *Fraser Forum*, July 2, 2009.

Jayati Ghosh — "Multidimensional Poverty in India," *Monthly Review*, September 4, 2010.

Andrew Grice — "Britain Faces Return to Victorian Levels of Poverty," *Independent* (UK), November 30, 2009.

Wayne Gum, Prabin Man Singh, and Beth Emmett — "Even the Himalayas Have Stopped Smiling: Climate Change, Poverty and Adaptation in Nepal," Oxfam International, August 2009. www.oxfam.org.

Kunal Kumar Kundu — "India's Poverty Curse," *Financial Times*, January 27, 2010.

Robert Rector — "Understanding Poverty in America: What the Census Bureau *Doesn't* Count When Reporting on the 'Poor,'" *National Review Online*, September 10, 2009. www.nationalreview.com.

Karen Fragala Smith — "Haiti: A Historical Perspective," *Newsweek*, January 15, 2010.

GLOBALVIEWPOINTS

CHAPTER 3

The Causes of Poverty

Poverty Around the World Is Caused by Government Intervention

Walter E. Williams

In the following viewpoint, Walter E. Williams argues that poverty is easy to explain. Williams rejects the explanations of poverty as resulting either from inadequate natural resources or from colonialism, citing counterexamples for each theory. Williams claims that there is a correlation between economic liberty and stronger protections of human rights all over the world. Williams contends that government protection of private property is one way that human rights are protected. He concludes that government intervention through collective ownership, high taxes, and income redistribution is what ultimately causes poverty, by reducing incentives that raise the productive capacity of individuals. Williams is a syndicated columnist and the John M. Olin Distinguished Professor of Economics at George Mason University.

As you read, consider the following questions:

1. According to Williams, what three explanations are there for why people or nations are poor?

2. What five examples of former colonies does the author give to refute the argument that colonialism causes poverty?

Walter E. Williams, "Poverty Is Easy to Explain," *The Freeman*, vol. 61, no. 4, May 2011. www.thefreemanonline.org. Copyright © 2011 by The Foundation for Economic Education. All rights reserved. Reproduced with permission.

3. What tax example does Williams give in support of the view that government taxation of property changes ownership characteristics?

Academics, politicians, clerics, and others always seem perplexed by the question: Why is there poverty? Answers usually range from exploitation and greed to slavery, colonialism, and other forms of immoral behavior. Poverty is seen as something to be explained with complicated analysis, conspiracy doctrines, and incantations. This vision of poverty is part of the problem in coming to grips with it.

Explanations for Poverty

There is very little either complicated or interesting about poverty. Poverty has been man's condition throughout his history. The causes of poverty are quite simple and straightforward. Generally, individual people or entire nations are poor for one or more of the following reasons: (1) they cannot produce many things highly valued by others; (2) they can produce things valued by others but they are prevented from doing so; or (3) they volunteer to be poor.

The true mystery is why there is any affluence at all. That is, how did a tiny proportion of man's population (mostly in the West) for only a tiny part of man's history (mainly in the nineteenth, twentieth, and twenty-first centuries) manage to escape the fate of their fellow men?

Sometimes, in reference to the United States, people point to its rich endowment of natural resources. This explanation is unsatisfactory. Were abundant natural resources the cause of affluence, Africa and South America would stand out as the richest continents, instead of being home to some of the world's most miserably poor people. By contrast, that explanation would suggest that resource-poor countries like Japan, Hong Kong, and Great Britain should be poor instead of ranking among the world's richest places.

Another unsatisfactory explanation of poverty is colonialism. This argument suggests that third-world poverty is a legacy of having been colonized, exploited, and robbed of its riches by the mother country. But it turns out that countries like the United States, Canada, Australia, and New Zealand were colonies; yet they are among the world's richest countries. Hong Kong was a colony of Great Britain until 1997, when China regained sovereignty, but it managed to become the second richest political jurisdiction in the Far East. On the other hand, Ethiopia, Liberia, Tibet, and Nepal were never colonies, or were so for only a few years, and they rank among the world's poorest and most backward countries.

Despite the many justified criticisms of colonialism and, I might add, multinationals, both served as a means of transferring Western technology and institutions, bringing backward peoples into greater contact with a more-developed Western world. A tragic fact is that many African countries have suffered significant decline since independence. In many of those countries the average citizen can boast that he ate more regularly and enjoyed greater human rights protections under colonial rule. The colonial powers never perpetrated the unspeakable human rights abuses, including genocide, that we have seen in post-independence Burundi, Uganda, Zimbabwe, Sudan, Central African Empire, Somalia, and elsewhere.

Those countries with greater economic liberty tend also to have stronger protections of human rights.

Economic Liberty and Human Rights

Any economist who suggests he has a complete answer to the causes of affluence should be viewed with suspicion. We do not know fully what makes some societies richer than others. However, we can make guesses based on correlations. Start out by ranking countries according to their economic systems. Conceptually we could arrange them from more capitalistic (having a larger free-market sector) to more communistic (with extensive State intervention and planning). Then consult Amnesty International's ranking of countries according to human rights abuses. Then get World Bank income statistics and rank countries from highest to lowest per capita income.

Compiling the three lists, one would observe a very strong, though imperfect, correlation: Those countries with greater economic liberty tend also to have stronger protections of human rights. And their people are wealthier. That finding is not a coincidence, so let us speculate on the relationship.

One way to gauge human rights protection is to ask to what extent the State protects voluntary exchange and private property. These signify the rights to acquire, keep, and dispose of property in any fashion so long as one does not violate the rights of others. The difference between private property rights and collectively held rights is not simply philosophical. Private property produces systemically different incentives and results from collective property.

Since collectivists often trivialize private property rights, they are worth elaborating. When property rights are held privately the costs and benefits of decisions are concentrated in the individual decision maker; with collectively held property rights they are dispersed across society. For example, private property forces homeowners to take into account the effect of their current decisions on the future value of their homes, because that value depends, among other things, on how long the property will provide housing services. Thus privately owned property holds one's personal wealth hostage to doing the socially responsible thing—economizing scarce resources.

Contrast these incentives to those of collective ownership. When the government owns the house, the individual has less incentive to take care of it simply because he does not capture the full benefit of his efforts. It is dispersed across society instead. The costs of neglecting the house are similarly spread.

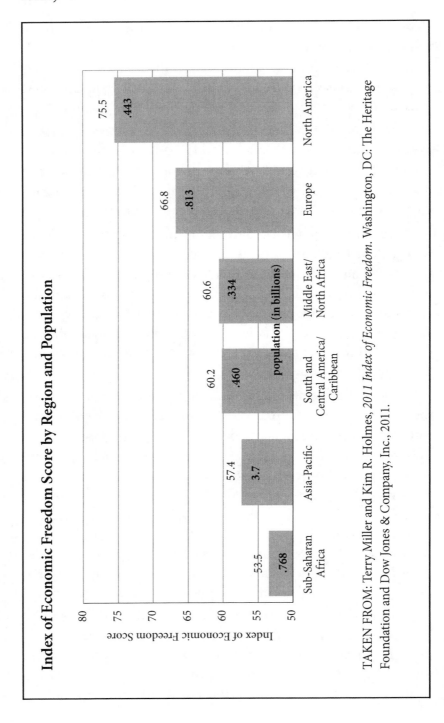

Index of Economic Freedom Score by Region and Population

North America 75.5 .443

Europe 66.8 .813

Middle East/North Africa 60.6 .334

South and Central America/Caribbean 60.2 .460

population (in billions)

Asia-Pacific 57.4 3.7

Sub-Saharan Africa 53.5 .768

Index of Economic Freedom Score

80 75 70 65 60 55 50

TAKEN FROM: Terry Miller and Kim R. Holmes, *2011 Index of Economic Freedom*. Washington, DC: The Heritage Foundation and Dow Jones & Company, Inc., 2011.

You do not have to be a rocket scientist to predict that under these circumstances less care will be taken.

Unwise Government Intervention

Nor is nominal collective ownership the only force that weakens social responsibility. When government taxes property, it changes the ownership characteristics. If government were to impose a 75 percent tax on a person selling his house, it would reduce his incentive to use the house wisely.

This argument applies to all activities, including work and investment. Whatever lowers the return from or raises the cost of an investment reduces incentives to make that investment in the first place. This applies to investment in human as well as physical capital—that is, those activities that raise the productive capacity of individuals.

To a significant degree the wealth of nations is embodied in their people. The starkest example of this is the experience of the Germans and Japanese after World War II. During the war, Allied bombing missions destroyed nearly the entire physical stock of each country. What was not destroyed was the human capital of the people: their skills and education. In two or three decades, both countries reemerged as formidable economic forces. The Marshall Plan and other U.S. subsidies to Europe and Japan cannot begin to explain their recovery.

If poverty is correctly seen as a result of the unwise government intervention and lack of productive capacity, more effective policy recommendations emerge.

Proper identification of the causes of poverty is critical. If it is seen, as is too often the case, as a result of exploitation, the policy recommendation that naturally emerges is income redistribution—that is, government confiscation of some people's "ill-gotten" gains and "restoration" to their "rightful" owners. This is the politics of envy: bigger and bigger welfare programs domestically and bigger and bigger foreign-aid programs internationally.

If poverty is correctly seen as a result of the unwise government intervention and lack of productive capacity, more effective policy recommendations emerge.

Poverty Is Alleviated by Active Citizenship and Effective Governments

Duncan Green

In the following viewpoint, Duncan Green argues that the key to eliminating poverty is allowing countries to democratically develop their own economic systems. Green contends that several examples of nations that were successful in combating poverty show that effective states can take many forms. What is important, he says, is that active social movements are involved in government, empowering people to use democracy to fight poverty. He cautions against external organizations imposing politics on poor countries or mandating particular economic frameworks. Green is head of research of Oxfam International in Great Britain and author of From Poverty to Power: How Active Citizens and Effective States Can Change the World.

As you read, consider the following questions:

1. According to Green, what country has been the world's fastest growing economy for the past three decades?
2. In 1900, the only country with a government elected by all its adult citizens was what country, according to the author?

Duncan Green, "Power v Poverty," *The New Statesman*, vol. 137, no. 4902, June 23, 2008, pp. 28–30. Copyright © 2008 by *The New Statesman*. All rights reserved. Reproduced by permission.

3. Which two countries does the author use as examples where countries have prospered economically despite having a strong central role for the state?

The global food-price crisis is exposing frightening levels of vulnerability in poor nations around the world. Yet these are countries into which the rich world, for half a century or more, has diverted hundreds of billions of dollars of humanitarian aid in pursuit of the high ideal of ending poverty. It is a good moment to take stock and ask what went wrong.

Haiti and Botswana

Compare two of the most vulnerable economies, Haiti and Botswana. In Haiti, spiralling food prices have in recent months [in 2008] prompted widespread rioting, claiming the lives of six people and forcing the resignation of the prime minister. This unrest has set back the search for political stability in an archetypal "fragile state". No such riots have occurred in the southern African nation of Botswana. In a country that imports 90 per cent of its food, soaring prices have undoubtedly hurt the poor, but the state has the money and capacity to help them cope.

Why does Haiti sink while Botswana swims? A landlocked state with a small population and an arid landscape, Botswana has a high dependence on diamonds—the very "curse of wealth" that has destabilized many other African countries. At independence in 1966, it had just two secondary schools and 12km [kilometers] of paved road, and relied on the UK [United Kingdom] for half of government revenues. Botswana ought to be a basket case.

But Botswana has become Africa's most enduring success story. Its GDP [gross domestic product] per capita has risen a hundredfold since independence. Over the past three decades it has been the world's fastest growing economy. It negotiated hard-fought deals for its diamonds with De Beers and used the royalties well. It has throughout remained one of sub-Saharan Africa's few non-racial democracies, despite being bordered (and occasionally invaded) by racist regimes in South Africa and Rhodesia.

The secret of Botswana's success lies in politics. The country's elite come from a single dominant ethnic group (the Batswana) whose governance systems, emphasising broad consultation and consensus building, emerged largely unscathed from colonialism. Botswana's leading human rights activist calls it "gentle authoritarianism". The government broke every rule in the so-called Washington consensus, setting up state-owned companies, nationalising mineral rights and steering the economy via six-year national development plans. "We are a free-market economy that does everything by planning," one local academic told me, laughing.

In the second half of the 20th century, dozens of developing countries emulated Botswana's success and achieved similar growth rates. "Getting the politics right" was key for them all. These countries have built effective states that guarantee the rule of law, ensure a healthy and educated population, control their national territories and create a positive environment for investment, growth and trade. For many, the growth spurt began with the redistribution of land and other assets.

Powerlessness and Poverty

This story bears little relation to the cruder theories of development advanced by rich-country governments or, for that matter, some NGOs [nongovernmental organisations]. Yet, getting the politics right really can "make poverty history". Aid alone cannot.

In many countries the state remains a work in progress and the rosy picture is not without flaws. Power battles and shifting alliances mean reverses are frequent. Raw power and gangsterism prevail in states that are more master than servant to their citizens. In his novel *Nineteen Eighty-Four*, written at the onset of the Cold War, George Orwell portrayed a totalitarian state built around the cult of Big Brother: "If you want a picture of the future, imagine a boot stamping on a human face—for ever." In the 20th century, some 170 million people were killed by their own governments, four times the number killed in wars between nations. But the worse deprivation and suffering now are not Orwellian in nature. They exist where states are weak: Half of all children who die before the age of five live in states defined as "fragile".

Getting the politics right really can "make poverty history".

Fixing this is not easy, but it can be done. Some states once branded as "failing" provide evidence. Malaysia went within a few decades from a post-independence meltdown of ethnic rioting to an industrial powerhouse. The economist Ha-Joon Chang points to his own country, South Korea, from where, in the 1960s, government officials were sent by the World Bank to Pakistan and the Philippines to "learn about good governance". The pupil swiftly outstripped the master.

If you define development merely as rising GDP per capita, then the story almost ends there—effective states create the basis for rapid growth. But development, particularly tackling poverty, is about far more than that. When the World Bank, in an unprecedented exercise, asked 64,000 poor people around the world about their lives, what emerged was a complex and human account of poverty, encompassing issues that are often ignored in the academic literature: the importance of being able to give one's children a good start in life, the mental anguish that poverty brings. The overall conclusion was that, "again and again, powerlessness seems to be at the core of the bad life".

Tackling such powerlessness is not just about election campaigns and government. Building "power within"—for example, women's assertiveness to insist on their right not to be beaten in the home—and "power with"—in the form of collective organisation—is essential to achieving the wider empowerment that transforms politics and societies.

In 1900, New Zealand was the only country with a government elected by all its adult citizens. By the end of the century, despite severe reversals, including fascism and communism, and succeeding waves of military coups against elected governments, there were ostensibly 120 electoral democracies in place. Democracies are often flawed and, as we have seen in several African countries, progress is reversible, but the overall trend remains positive.

Democracies are often flawed and, as we have seen in several African countries, progress is reversible, but the overall trend remains positive.

Active Citizenship and Efficient Governments

Effective states in East Asia and elsewhere have typically taken off under autocracies. In Latin America, active social movements and political organisations have rarely been accompanied by effective states. Does this mean active citizenship and efficient governments are mutually exclusive? Happily, the evidence suggests that the "Asian values" argument for benign dictatorship, once espoused by leaders in Singapore and Malaysia, is wrong. A recent survey by the Harvard economist Dani Rodrik found that democracies produce more predictable long-run growth rates, greater short-term stability and more equality, and are better able to handle economic shocks.

Many of the countries that have had active citizens and been run efficiently have already ceased to be poor and disappeared off the development radar. Some of the most successful transformations in the past century, such as those of Sweden and Finland, have been triggered by social pacts within a democracy, showing what the combination of activism and good government can achieve.

Yet, though this combination is at the heart of development, it is seldom acknowledged in debates about the "development industry", typified by international institutions such as the World Bank and the IMF [International Monetary Fund]. Here, economic policy is king, and politics is often seen as an irritating process through which unworthy individuals use their power to unravel the plans of wise economists. "Getting the prices right" requires the state to get out of economic management, freeing the stage for the true heroes of development: the entrepreneurs.

It hasn't worked. The retreat of the state in Latin America, once a faithful devotee of Washington consensus prescriptions, failed to lead to lasting progress. Meanwhile, countries such as China and Vietnam, which maintained a central role for the state, prospered.

The importance of politics in development will only grow. The world is entering a new age of scarcity, in which food, water and carbon are rationed, either explicitly, through regulation, or implicitly, by price. In this environment, conflicts over access to basic resources are bound to intensify. Politics and power will decide who gets what.

All this poses challenges to the $100bn global development industry. Official donors such as the UK's Department for International Development are trying to reassess their thinking to understand better the role of politics in development. But they face a dilemma: Any outside body, especially a government institution, interferes with domestic politics in developing countries at its peril. To get round this, there is always a temptation to turn political issues into technical ones—for example, by focusing on "governance" or "institution-building". But, by failing to confront issues of power, such approaches often give rise to the same frustrations as those that focus on economic policy: Why won't these countries do what's good for them?

The Importance of Empowerment

International organisations such as Oxfam [International] have long been criticised by some developing-country partner organisations for preferring policy to politics. But they face real limits. Charity law, mission and bitter experience should dissuade them from becoming mere support groups for any political party in a given developing country. Instead, they have to promote empowerment without becoming politicised. It is a fine line to tread, but it is eminently feasible.

In Bolivia, for example, 20 years of support for the Chiquitano Indians helped them move from semi-slavery to becoming a political force, with the founding of indigenous people's organisations, such as that led by José Bailaba, and the election of Chiquitano mayors and senators. Following the election of South America's first indigenous president, Evo Morales, a land reform bill gave the Chiquitanos rights to a million hectares of traditional lands.

Rich-country governments and their citizens need to ensure that this system of global government supports national development efforts based on the state and its people working together.

Even though the alchemy of development takes place primarily in the crucible of effective states with active citizens, global institutions such as aid donors, the UN [United Nations] and transnational corporations play a significant role.

Nation-states will not wither away, even if their actions are constrained by an ever-growing web of global and regional trade agreements, bilateral investment treaties and the proliferating "soft law" of international conventions and codes of conduct on everything from financial services to human rights. Rich-country governments and their citizens need to ensure that this system of global government supports national development efforts based on the state and its people working together. They must also deter powerful countries and corporations from doing harm, whether through paying bribes or imposing policies that hurt the poor.

The fight against poverty, inequality and environmental collapse will define the 21st century, as the fight against slavery or for universal suffrage defined earlier eras. It is hard to imagine a more worthwhile cause.

High Birth Rates and Population Growth Are Correlated with Poverty

United Nations Population Fund (UNPFA)

In the following viewpoint, the United Nations Population Fund (UNPFA) argues that having smaller families improves economic prospects not only on the family level but also on countries as a whole. UNPFA suggests that low use of contraception in developing countries inhibits efforts to reduce poverty. UNPFA concludes that improving access to contraception and family planning in poor countries would have many positive effects, including the alleviation of poverty. UNPFA is an international development agency that promotes the right of every woman, man, and child to enjoy a life of health and equal opportunity.

As you read, consider the following questions:

1. According to UNPFA, how many women worldwide would like to delay or prevent pregnancy but are not using effective contraception?

2. What is the average number of births for the poorest fifth of women in fifty-six developing countries, according to the author?

3. To what do studies attribute up to one-quarter of the "miracle growth" of East Asia after 1960, according to UNPFA?

For the past seven decades, high fertility and poverty have been strongly correlated, and the world's poorest countries also have the highest fertility and population growth rates. To some extent, this is due to the fact that poverty and its determinants (subsistence agriculture, low levels of education, subordinate position of women) also tend to perpetuate high fertility.

But there is also a causal link in the opposite direction, with lower fertility leading to less poverty. True, lower birth rates, a major component of population growth, do not, by themselves, guarantee greater prosperity. But they do make economic gains more feasible.

The Benefits of Lower Birth Rates

Family planning allows women to delay childbearing so they can complete their education, participate in the labour force while acquiring skills and experience. Improving the health, education and prospects of women and adolescent girls acts as an economic stimulus for countries, and has strong intergeneration benefits.

Longer intervals between births also significantly improve child and maternal health, generating benefits over children's entire life course. Having fewer, healthier children can reduce the economic burden on poor families and allow them to invest more in each child's care and schooling, helping to break the cycle of poverty.

Even over shorter time intervals, in the order of 2–5 years, it has been shown that smaller households, with fewer dependent members, experience higher upward economic mobility and rise out of temporary poverty spells more quickly than larger households with more dependent members.

In a more immediate way, lower fertility changes the proportion of economically active versus inactive family household members, so that approximately the same income has to be divided with fewer dependent household members. Although this effect is somewhat mechanical, it has been shown to have a major impact on poverty rates, when defined in conventional terms of per capita income or consumption.

Having fewer, healthier children can reduce the economic burden on poor families and allow them to invest more in each child's care and schooling, helping to break the cycle of poverty.

At the aggregate level, lower population growth may reduce the pressure on social infrastructure and the need for social investments. Very high fertility rates are characteristic of the least developed countries, those countries that are least able to invest in health and education. High population growth contributes to a vicious cycle of poverty, illiteracy, poor health and high mortality.

Over the longer term, smaller families can change the age structures of countries. As fertility begins to decline, so too does the number of dependents relative to workers. When the working population is relatively large and policies foster job creation, countries can build human and physical capital. The greater number of people in the workforce compared to the number of dependents allows for greater saving and investment. However, economists caution that these benefits are not automatic and that they depend on appropriate institutional environments.

In addition, rapid population growth contributes to an increase of inequality. This is because an abundant supply of labour tends to lower the price of labour with respect to capital and land. Increasing inequality nearly always implies greater poverty as well.

The ability to plan how many children to have and when to have them is a recognized human right. However, universal access to contraceptives is not yet a reality—especially among the poorest. Worldwide, 215 million women would like to delay or prevent pregnancy, but are not using effective contraception. Simply meeting this 'unmet need' for contraception would go a long way toward lowering fertility.

Demand for family planning is expected to soar in the next 15 years as millions of young people become sexually active and smaller families become the norm in many countries. But funding for family planning is only a fraction of what is needed.

As most developing countries now recognize, committed and focused policies and programmes are urgently needed to moderate population growth as quickly as possible, thus enhancing economic growth and easing demands on social services.

Get the Facts

Some 215 million women who would like to delay childbearing still have no access to contraception. Many of them live in the poorest countries, where governments are having trouble building schools and health systems for their rapidly growing populations.

Four in 10 of the 186 million pregnancies that occur in developing countries each year are unintended, meaning that they were unwanted or were not wanted at the time. Women who lack access to effective contraception account for 82 per cent of all unintended pregnancies.

It has been estimated that in some middle-income countries like Honduras and Colombia the effect on poverty of avoiding all unwanted births would be of the same magnitude as the conditional transfer programs that the governments of those countries are using as their main policy instrument for combating poverty.

The Benefits of Planned Pregnancies

Helping women and couples have healthy, wanted pregnancies helps achieve social and economic gains beyond the health sector . . . through higher educational attainment, especially for women; higher labor productivity, including greater female labor force participation; and greater accumulation of household wealth through savings and investment, which helps to meet the MDG [Millennium Development Goal] of reducing poverty. Environmental benefits also accrue for future generations when couples have smaller families, lowering population growth and related consumption of scarce natural resources.

Susheela Singh et al.,
"Adding It Up: The Costs and Benefits of Investing
in Family Planning and Maternal and Newborn Health,"
Guttmacher Institute and United Nations Population Fund, 2009.

In 56 developing countries, the poorest fifth of women still average six births, compared to 3.2 in the wealthiest quintile.

The benefits of fully meeting the need for both family planning and maternal and newborn health services in developing countries would be dramatic. Roughly doubling the current global investments in family planning and pregnancy-related care, from $11.8 billion to $24.6 billion, would reduce:

- maternal deaths by more than two-thirds, from 356,000 to 105,000;

- newborn deaths by more than half, from 3.2 million to 1.5 million;

- unintended pregnancies by more than two-thirds, from 75 million to 22 million;

- unsafe abortions by almost three-quarters, from 20 million to 5.5 million; and

- deaths from unsafe abortion by more than four-fifths, from 46,000 to 8,000.

Studies attribute about one-quarter of the 'miracle growth' in East Asia after 1960 and one-third of the increase in per capita income to a demographic 'bonus': a larger percentage of workers compared to dependents, resulting from fertility declines. In many countries of Africa, where fertility remains high, the dependency ratio has not yet begun to decline.

Reproductive health issues, most of them related to pregnancy and childbirth, result in 250 million years of productive life lost each year.

Brazilian economists have demonstrated that had fertility in Brazil not diminished during the 1946–1996 period, economic growth would have needed to be 0.4% per year higher in order to achieve the same poverty reduction that the country experienced during these years.

Although most of the least developed countries have policies to lower fertility, contraceptive prevalence remains low in countries with high fertility, most of which are located in sub-Saharan Africa. In much of this region, social norms still favour large families.

Reproductive health issues, most of them related to pregnancy and childbirth, result in 250 million years of productive life lost each year and reduce the productivity of women by 20 per cent.

Population Growth Is Not the Cause of Poverty

Nicholas Eberstadt

In the following viewpoint, Nicholas Eberstadt argues that it is a waste of money to attempt to control population growth as a solution to poverty. Eberstadt claims that government policies that thwart growth and freedom, not increasing numbers of people, are what make people in certain countries poor. Eberstadt contends that efforts by international organizations to improve health, literacy, and voluntary contraception in poor countries are beneficial in their own right, but he denies that these efforts reduce birth rates—thereby reducing poverty—as some groups claim. Eberstadt is the Henry Wendt Scholar in Political Economy at the American Enterprise Institute for Public Policy Research. He is the author of The Poverty of "The Poverty Rate": Measure and Mismeasure of Want in Modern America.

As you read, consider the following questions:

1. According to Eberstadt, what two prosperous countries are both densely populated and poor in resources?
2. The average real price of grain has been falling by what percentage per decade, according to the author?
3. Which two countries cut fertility rates by more than half in the same quarter century, according to Eberstadt?

President [Barack] Obama has ended the ban on federal funds imposed by the [George W.] Bush administration on groups that promote or perform abortions abroad and on the United Nations Population Fund [UNFPA]. He must take this opportunity to put pressure on the UNFPA to concentrate on the health of women and babies—and to stop wasting money assaulting the poor with wrongheaded population-control schemes.

Population and Poverty

"Continued rapid population growth poses a bigger threat to poverty reduction in most countries than HIV/AIDS," the UNFPA said in a hysterical statement on World Population Day, last July [2008]. This is plain wrong: It is not human numbers that cause poverty, but bad economic policies, laws and institutions.

The densely populated Netherlands and Japan are prosperous but poor in resources, while much of impoverished Africa is thinly populated but rich in resources. The United States rose to affluence with one of the world's highest long-term population growth rates, while now-prosperous Ireland had negative long-term rates. Clearly, neither human numbers nor natural resources are keys to the modern story of global wealth and poverty.

It is not human numbers that cause poverty, but bad economic policies, laws and institutions.

The UNFPA talks of "women's empowerment and gender equality" and "universal access to reproductive health" but, despite this politically correct discourse, it remains committed to its original purpose of reducing population growth: Reproductive healthcare is "the most practicable option for slowing population growth," it says, equating this with poverty, food insecurity and environmental degradation.

The Adverse Effects of Population Growth

The adverse effects of population growth can easily be confused with other factors, because rapid population growth often occurs along with other forces that reduce human well-being. For example, rapid population growth is common in many tropical areas of the world. Yet tropical environments themselves retard human productive activity due to heat, endemic disease, and poor soils. It would be easy to conclude that fast population growth lowers productivity, when actually the tropical environment may be the cause.

Seth W. Norton,
"Population Growth, Economic Freedom, and the Rule of Law,"
PERC Policy Series, PS-24, February 2002.

These fallacies hark back to the 18th-century economist Thomas Robert Malthus. Like many other pressure groups and NGOs [nongovernmental organizations], the UNFPA continues to commit elementary analytical errors: ignoring evidence staring us in the face.

The 20th century saw human numbers quadruple to more than six billion but food production widely outstripped population growth, average life expectancy doubled to well over 60 years, while global GDP [gross domestic product] per capita more than quintupled.

In the 1960s, alarmists such as Paul Ehrlich predicted imminent mass famine around the world. Indeed, in the last couple of years global food prices briefly shot up—maize, wheat and rice all doubled or tripled in a short time—but fell back again. In fact, the long-term trend in real grain prices over the past century has been heading steadily downward, at an average of seven to 10 percent per decade (depending on the product).

To be sure, a horrifying number of people today still live in squalor, scourged by disease and hunger—but the correct name for this is poverty, not "overpopulation." In countries where people cannot securely own property, cannot sell their produce freely and get scant protection in law, government is poverty's handmaiden.

Only economic growth and freedom, not deceitful population programs from the [United Nations Population Fund], can empower women and spare them poverty and premature death.

Government Intervention in Population Control

Population alarmists and their allies in the UN are deluding themselves when they claim government intervention can reduce fertility rates and "stabilize" population. Their mantra is that education, high literacy and cheap birth control lead to lower birth rates.

Health, literacy and voluntary contraception are meritorious objectives in their own right, irrespective of any influence on population growth. But it is misleading to claim they predictably reduce birth rates.

Take literacy. The adult literacy rate in 2006 was about a third higher in Malawi than Morocco (54% vs. 40%), yet fertility levels in Malawi were double. Family planning campaigns are similarly unpredictable: In 1974 Mexico started a vigorous campaign to cut population growth and got fertility levels down by 56% but Brazil's fertility level fell by 54% with no campaign at all, in the same quarter century. These are not cherry-picked examples: There is simply no way of knowing in advance the impact of family planning programs on birth rates.

It turns out that the single best international predictor of fertility levels is the number of children that women say they would like. The only proven way of curbing population growth is coercion, as in India briefly in the 1970s and in UNFPA-client China today. There is no other assured way of accomplishing immediate and dramatic birth reductions through population policy—period.

Many organizations, including the World Health Organization and UNICEF [the United Nations Children's Fund], already work to promote the health of women and children internationally. Plainly, many global health threats, from maternal and neonatal deaths to diarrhea, malaria and other infectious diseases, are creations of poverty. Only economic growth and freedom, not deceitful population programs from the UNFPA, can empower women and spare them poverty and premature death.

Hunger Is Both a Cause of and a Consequence of Poverty

World Food Programme

In the following viewpoint, the World Food Programme argues that hunger is tightly linked with poverty. The World Food Programme claims that hunger and poverty create a vicious cycle—a hunger-poverty trap, where hunger leads to poverty and poverty leads to food insecurity and hunger. The World Food Programme contends that the bulk of the world's hungry poor live in rural areas but that the number of hungry poor in urban areas is growing due to migration and high food prices. The World Food Programme, part of the United Nations system, is the world's largest humanitarian agency fighting hunger worldwide.

As you read, consider the following questions:

1. According to the World Food Programme, how many undernourished people were there in developing countries in 2008?

2. Which two continents account for more than 90 percent of the world's hungry, according to the author?

3. According to the World Food Programme, evidence shows that who pays more for food: the rich or the poor?

Severe hunger is life defining. It wrecks people's health, reduces their productivity, diminishes their learning capacity, overcomes their sense of hope and upsets their overall well-being. Lack of food stunts growth, saps energy and hinders foetal development. Hungry people's constant struggle to secure food consumes valuable time and energy, reducing their possibilities of receiving education and finding alternative sources of income.

Worldwide, there were 848 million undernourished people in 2003–2005. The undernourished population in developing countries increased from 824 million in 1990–1992 to 832 million in 2003–2005. Although this was a relatively small increase, the long-term trend is worrying, as high food prices increased the number by 75 million in 2007 and 40 million in 2008, when it reached 963 million. This jeopardizes the prospect of reaching the Millennium Development Goal (MDG) of halving the proportion of hungry people worldwide by 2015.

No statistic can embody the sheer terror of hunger. For hundreds of millions of people, hunger is a fact of life that imperils their health, reduces their productivity and diminishes their educational attainment.

Food Insecurity and Hunger

Hunger is an outcome of food insecurity, which in turn is often caused by poverty. Understanding hunger and its causes depends on identifying the necessary conditions for food security. The 1996 World Food Summit defined food security as: "Food security exists when all people, at all times, have physical and economic access to sufficient, safe and nutritious food to meet their dietary needs and preferences for an active and healthy life." It involves four aspects: availability, access, utilization and stability.

Identification of the factors necessary for food security has fostered a new, more heterogeneous conception of hunger. A seminal work by Amartya Sen proposed that famines, hunger and malnutrition are related less to declines in food availability than to people's access to food. Sen demonstrated that during famines in Bengal (1943), Ethiopia (1973) and Bangladesh (1974) food availability did not decline significantly—and sometimes it even increased. These famines were caused by such factors as falling wages, rising food prices, loss of employment and declining livestock prices, all of which relate to the food access dimension—and to markets. Lack of food availability is neither a sufficient nor a necessary condition for famines or hunger.

Hunger is an outcome of food insecurity, which in turn is often caused by poverty.

Sen's analysis is relevant in today's environment of high food prices. Although food is available, many households cannot afford the same quantity and quality as before, because incomes have not kept up with prices.

Markets play a role in many of the dimensions of hunger and food insecurity.

The Hunger-Poverty Trap

Hunger is the bottom line of poverty, and food is central to poor people's concerns. Poverty and hunger are not easy to disentangle. Not all poor people are hungry, and malnutrition, such as micronutrient deficiencies, also occurs among the non-poor. However, all hungry people are considered poor. Hunger is an intergenerational phenomenon passed from mother to child. An undernourished mother generally passes the condition on to her child as low birth weight, which has an impact on the child's future health and well-being. This process is known as the "hunger trap".

Hunger traps are linked to poverty conditions. Poverty and hunger are interlinked and mutually reinforcing; hunger is not only a cause of poverty, but also its consequence. Development economists [such as Ragnar Nurkse] recognized this phenomenon half a century ago: "[A] poor man may not have enough to eat; being underfed, his health may be weak; being physically weak, his working capacity is low, which means that he is poor, which in turn means he will not have enough to eat; and so on." Hunger and poverty drive each other in a vicious cycle, generating a hunger-poverty trap. The impact of hunger on health, education and productivity is long term, which reinforces the hunger-poverty trap. The damage done by malnutrition before the age of 24 months is irreversible, making escape from the hunger-poverty trap difficult. This not only hampers individuals, but also imposes a crushing economic burden on the developing world. Economists estimate that the cost of child hunger and undernutrition can amount to as much as 11 percent of a country's gross domestic product (GDP).

Several factors can contribute to a hunger-poverty trap, including shocks related to diseases or weather, lack of assets and institutions, risks, small-scale and physical isolation, all of which affect access to markets and transaction costs.

Poverty and hunger are interlinked and mutually reinforcing; hunger is not only a cause of poverty, but also its consequence.

The Hungry Poor

Lack of access to markets, assets, technology, infrastructure, health facilities and schools breeds hunger. So does women's exclusion from land, education, decision making and mobility—a situation that is reinforced by laws and/or cultural norms in many places. Higher malnutrition tends to be concentrated in remote, resource-poor rural areas. This indicates that visible and invisible barriers to access to productive assets, or "asset poverty", are important drivers of high hunger and poverty levels. An uneven initial distribution of assets is important in generating and perpetuating poverty and hunger traps. The initial distribution of assets and the asset base of households matter because households use their assets to increase their wealth and well-being. The access of groups that are marginalized or discriminated against, including indigenous peoples and ethnic minorities, might be compromised.

"Poor and hungry people often face social and political exclusion, unable to demand their rights. They have little access to education, health services, and safe drinking water" [United Nations Millennium Project Task Force on Hunger, 2005]. They suffer an extreme lack of economic, political or social freedom and choice. These deprivations are deep-rooted and prevent poor people from lifting themselves out of the trap. It is difficult to discuss hunger without discussing poverty. Hence, the focus on the *hungry poor*. . . .

Hunger may be expected where widespread asset deprivation, of land, education and financial and social capital, and underinvestment in technology, infrastructure and institutions prevent poor households from increasing their incomes. The hungry poor are stuck in a poverty trap of low productivity, high transaction costs and poor access to markets.

The hungry poor are stuck in a poverty trap of low productivity, high transaction costs and poor access to markets.

The Rural Poor

Global numbers on hunger hide regional variations. Asia and Africa contain more than 90 percent of the world's hungry, with China and India accounting for 42 percent and sub-Saharan Africa for a quarter. Although undernourishment has declined in South Asia, this region still has the highest overall prevalence of underweight children in the world, at 42 percent of all those under 5. Sub-Saharan Africa ranks a distant second with 28 percent.

Aggregate numbers do not provide a comprehensive understanding of what poverty and hunger mean, who the hungry poor are and where they live. It is a bitter irony that 75 percent of the world's hungry poor live in rural areas, where most people are engaged in agricultural activities. Although they produce food, these people are vulnerable to risks associated with economic, weather-related and other shocks, and are unable to grow or buy enough food to meet their families' requirements. According to the United Nations Millennium Project Task Force on Hunger (2005): "estimates indicate that the majority of hungry people live in rural areas. The task force believes that about half of the hungry are smallholder farming households unable either to grow or to buy enough food to meet the family's requirements. . . . We estimate that roughly two-tenths of the hungry are landless rural people. A smaller group, perhaps one-tenth of the hungry, are pastoralists, fisher folk, and people who depend on forests for their livelihoods. . . . The remaining share of the hungry, around two-tenths, live in urban areas."

Poverty is more extensive and deeper in rural areas.

Rural poverty is often greatest in areas furthest away from roads, markets, schools and health services. For example, a survey in the United Republic of Tanzania found a significant correlation between child nutrition status and access to major roads. . . . Areas where transportation costs are high—more than US$1.5 per metric ton kilometer (MTkm)—generally have a high prevalence of underweight children. Where roads and infrastructure are present and well connected, as in southern Africa, the prevalence of underweight children is low. These associations suggest the existence of geographical poverty traps.

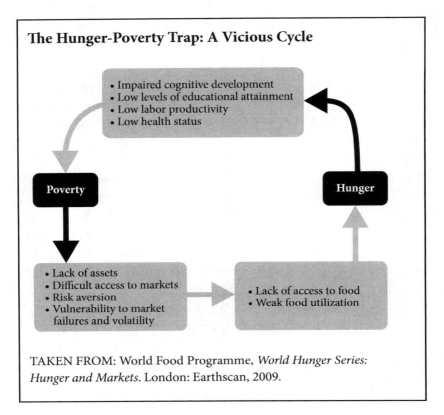

The Hunger-Poverty Trap: A Vicious Cycle

- Impaired cognitive development
- Low levels of educational attainment
- Low labor productivity
- Low health status

Poverty

Hunger

- Lack of assets
- Difficult access to markets
- Risk aversion
- Vulnerability to market failures and volatility

- Lack of access to food
- Weak food utilization

TAKEN FROM: World Food Programme, *World Hunger Series: Hunger and Markets*. London: Earthscan, 2009.

Underweight rates in rural areas of developing countries are on average twice those of urban areas. This is linked to lower access to health services, safe water and sanitation in rural areas. In Burundi, for example, skilled health personnel attend 83 percent of births in urban areas, but only 16 percent in rural areas. Dietary quality is also much lower in rural than in urban areas.

This does not mean that there are no hungry poor in urban areas. In fact, poverty is tending to become increasingly urbanized because of high levels of migration by poor people from rural areas. However, poverty remains highly concentrated in rural areas. A higher proportion of poor people live in rural areas, and of the people living in rural areas, a higher proportion are poor. Poverty is more extensive and deeper in rural areas.

High Food Prices

Urban populations can face food access challenges because they depend on markets and often tackle difficult trade-offs among competing demands on their income, such as housing, health or transport, which may be more expensive in urban areas. The urban poor are particularly vulnerable to high food prices. The 1997/1998 financial crisis in Indonesia, for example, showed that micronutrient deficiencies can grow rapidly in urban areas when staple food prices increase. Across the world, high food prices have helped provoke demonstrations and riots in urban areas, where political mobilization is much easier. Only careful monitoring can tell whether the impact of high food prices on nutrition is worse in urban than in rural areas.

There is evidence that poor people pay higher prices than rich people. The reasons are not clear, but could be related to market failures, including market power, poor market integration and lack of credit in remote areas, forcing poor households to buy goods in small quantities and during the lean season at higher prices.

To address global hunger efficiently, its local manifestations must be taken into account. The heterogeneous character of the hungry poor demands consideration of their specific natural, political, cultural, religious and socioeconomic environments.

Hunger and poverty are deeper and more extensive in rural areas. Whether or not high food prices and the global financial crisis will change this pattern needs to be monitored carefully. Maintaining a focus on the hungry poor and the specific obstacles they face is a key to breaking the cycle of hunger and poverty across the developing world.

Poverty Is Not Clearly Linked with Hunger

Abhijit Banerjee and Esther Duflo

In the following viewpoint, Abhijit Banerjee and Esther Duflo argue that the link between poverty and hunger is more complicated than is generally thought. Banerjee and Duflo contend that statistics showing lowered consumption of calories do not necessarily indicate increased hunger. They posit that people have enough to eat and may voluntarily be forgoing calories in order to spend their money on other items. The authors' research causes them to deny that there is a hunger-based poverty trap, where a lack of food keeps people poor. Banerjee is the Ford Foundation International Professor of Economics, and Duflo is the Abdul Latif Jameel Professor of Poverty Alleviation and Development Economics, in the Department of Economics at the Massachusetts Institute of Technology.

As you read, consider the following questions:

1. According to Banerjee and Duflo, what fraction of the population in India lives in households where per capita calorie consumption is less than the minimum requirements?

2. The authors claim that the poor could spend up to 30 percent more on food if it cut out spending on what three items?

3. According to the authors, total educational attainment in central and southern Africa would increase by 7.5 percent if every mother did what?

For many in the West, poverty is almost synonymous with hunger. Indeed, the announcement by the United Nations Food and Agriculture Organization in 2009 that more than 1 billion people are suffering from hunger grabbed headlines in a way that any number of World Bank estimates of how many poor people live on less than a dollar a day never did.

But is it really true? Are there really more than a billion people going to bed hungry each night? Our research on this question has taken us to rural villages and teeming urban slums around the world, collecting data and speaking with poor people about what they eat and what else they buy, from Morocco to Kenya, Indonesia to India. We've also tapped into a wealth of insights from our academic colleagues. What we've found is that the story of hunger, and of poverty more broadly, is far more complex than any one statistic or grand theory; it is a world where those without enough to eat may save up to buy a TV instead, where more money doesn't necessarily translate into more food, and where making rice cheaper can sometimes even lead people to buy less rice. . . .

Poverty and Hunger

The international community has certainly bought into the idea that poverty traps exist—and that they are the reason that millions are starving. The first U.N. [United Nations] Millennium Development Goal, for instance, is to "eradicate extreme poverty and hunger." In many countries, the definition of poverty itself has been connected to food; the thresholds for determining that someone was poor were originally calculated as the budget necessary to buy a certain number of calories, plus some other indispensable purchases, such as housing. A "poor" person has essentially been classified as someone without enough to eat.

So it is no surprise that government efforts to help the poor are largely based on the idea that the poor desperately need food and that quantity is what matters. Food subsidies are ubiquitous in the Middle East: Egypt spent $3.8 billion on food subsidies in the 2008 fiscal year, some 2 percent of its GDP [gross domestic product]. Indonesia distributes subsidized rice. Many states in India have a similar program. In the state of Orissa, for example, the poor are entitled to 55 pounds of rice a month at about 1 rupee per pound, less than 20 percent of the market price. Currently, the Indian Parliament is debating a Right to Food Act, which would allow people to sue the government if they are starving. Delivering such food aid is a logistical nightmare. In India it is estimated that more than half of the wheat and one-third of the rice gets "lost" along the way. To support direct food aid in this circumstance, one would have to be quite convinced that what the poor need more than anything is more grain.

A "poor" person has essentially been classified as someone without enough to eat.

But what if the poor are not, in general, eating too little food? What if, instead, they are eating the wrong kinds of food, depriving them of nutrients needed to be successful, healthy adults? What if the poor aren't starving, but choosing to spend their money on other priorities? Development experts and policy makers would have to completely reimagine the way they think about hunger. And governments and aid agencies would need to stop pouring money into failed programs and focus instead on finding new ways to truly improve the lives of the world's poorest.

A Decline in Consumption

Consider India, one of the great puzzles in this age of food crises. The standard media story about the country, at least when it comes to food, is about the rapid rise of obesity and diabetes as the urban upper-middle class gets richer. Yet the real story of nutrition in India over the last quarter century, as Princeton professor Angus Deaton and Jean Drèze, a professor at Allahabad University and a special advisor to the Indian government, have shown, is not that Indians are becoming fatter: It is that they are in fact eating less and less. Despite the country's rapid economic growth, per capita calorie consumption in India has declined; moreover, the consumption of all other nutrients except fat also appears to have gone down among all groups, even the poorest. Today, more than three-quarters of the population live in households whose per capita calorie consumption is less than 2,100 calories in urban areas and 2,400 in rural areas—numbers that are often cited as "minimum requirements" in India for those engaged in manual labor. Richer people still eat more than poorer people. But at all levels of income, the share of the budget devoted to food has declined and people consume fewer calories.

What is going on? The change is not driven by declining incomes; by all accounts, Indians are making more money than ever before. Nor is it because of rising food prices—between the early 1980s and 2005, food prices declined relative to the prices of other things, both in rural and urban India. Although food prices have increased again since 2005, Indians began eating less precisely when the price of food was going down.

So the poor, even those whom the FAO [Food and Agriculture Organization of the United Nations] would classify as hungry on the basis of what they eat, do not seem to want to eat much more even when they can. Indeed, they seem to be eating less. What could explain this? Well, to start, let's assume that the poor know what they are doing. After all, they are the ones who eat and work. If they could be tremendously more productive and earn much more by eating more, then they probably would. So could it be that eating more doesn't actually make us particularly more productive, and as a result, there is no nutrition-based poverty trap?

One reason the poverty trap might not exist is that most people have enough to eat. We live in a world today that is theoretically capable of feeding every person on the planet. In 1996, the FAO estimated that world food production was enough to provide at least 2,700 calories per person per day. Starvation still exists, but only as a result of the way food gets shared among us. There is no absolute scarcity. Using price data from the Philippines, we calculated the cost of the cheapest diet sufficient to give 2,400 calories. It would cost only about 21 cents a day, very affordable even for the very poor (the worldwide poverty line is set at roughly a dollar per day). The catch is, it would involve eating only bananas and eggs, something no one would like to do day in, day out. But so long as people are prepared to eat bananas and eggs when they need to, we should find very few people stuck in poverty because they do not get enough to eat. Indian surveys bear this out: The percentage of people who say they do not have enough food has dropped dramatically over time, from 17 percent in 1983 to 2 percent in 2004. So, perhaps people eat less because they are less hungry.

One reason the poverty trap might not exist is that most people have enough to eat.

And perhaps they are really less hungry, despite eating fewer calories. It could be that because of improvements in water and sanitation, they are leaking fewer calories in bouts of diarrhea and other ailments. Or maybe they are less hungry because of the decline of heavy physical work. With the availability of drinking water in villages, women do not need to carry heavy loads for long distances; improvements in transportation have reduced the need to travel on foot; in even the poorest villages, flour is now milled using a motorized mill, instead of women grinding it by hand. Using the average calorie requirements calculated by the Indian Council of Medical Research, Deaton and Drèze note that the decline in calorie consumption over the last quarter century could be entirely explained by a modest decrease in the number of people engaged in heavy physical work.

Choices About Spending

Beyond India, one hidden assumption in our description of the poverty trap is that the poor eat as much as they can. If there is any chance that by eating a bit more the poor could start doing meaningful work and get out of the poverty trap zone, then they should eat as much as possible. Yet most people living on less than a dollar a day do not seem to act as if they are starving. If they were, surely they would put every available penny into buying more calories. But they do not. In an 18-country data set we assembled on the lives of the poor, food represents 36 to 79 percent of consumption among the rural extremely poor, and 53 to 74 percent among their urban counterparts.

It is not because they spend all the rest on other necessities. In Udaipur, India, for example, we find that the typical poor household could spend up to 30 percent more on food, if it completely cut expenditures on alcohol, tobacco, and festivals. The poor seem to have many choices, and they don't choose to spend as much as they can on food. Equally remarkable is that even the money that people do spend on food is not spent to maximize the intake of calories or micronutrients. Studies have shown that when very poor people get a chance to spend a little bit more on food, they don't put everything into getting more calories. Instead, they buy better-tasting, more expensive calories.

In one study conducted in two regions of China, researchers offered randomly selected poor households a large subsidy on the price of the basic staple (wheat noodles in one region, rice in the other). We usually expect that when the price of something goes down, people buy more of it. The opposite happened. Households that received subsidies for rice or wheat consumed less of those two foods and ate more shrimp and meat, even though their staples now cost less. Overall, the calorie intake of those who received the subsidy did not increase (and may even have decreased), despite the fact that their purchasing power had increased. Nor did the nutritional content improve in any other sense. The likely reason is that because the rice and wheat noodles were cheap but not particularly tasty, feeling richer might actually have made them consume less of those staples. This reasoning suggests that at least among these very poor urban households, getting more calories was not a priority: Getting better-tasting ones was.

All told, many poor people might eat fewer calories than we—or the FAO—think is appropriate. But this does not seem to be because they have no other choice; rather, they are not hungry enough to seize every opportunity to eat more. So perhaps there aren't a billion "hungry" people in the world after all.

The Hunger-Based Poverty Trap

None of this is to say that the logic of the hunger-based poverty trap is flawed. The idea that better nutrition would propel someone on the path to prosperity was almost surely very important at some point in history, and it may still be today. Nobel Prize–winning economic historian Robert Fogel calculated that in Europe during the Middle Ages and the Renaissance, food production did not provide enough calories to sustain a full working population. This could explain why there were large numbers of beggars—they were literally incapable of any work. The pressure of just getting enough food to survive seems to have driven some people to take rather extreme steps. There was an epidemic of witch killing in Europe during the Little Ice Age (from the mid-1500s to 1800), when crop failures were common and fish was less abundant. Even today, Tanzania experiences a rash of such killings whenever there is a drought—a convenient way to get rid of an unproductive mouth to feed at times when resources are very tight. Families, it seems, suddenly discover that an older woman living with them (usually a grandmother) is a witch, after which she gets chased away or killed by others in the village.

But the world we live in today is for the most part too rich for the occasional lack of food to be a big part of the story of the persistence of poverty on a large scale. This is of course different during natural or man-made disasters, or in famines that kill and weaken millions. As Nobel laureate Amartya Sen has shown, most recent famines have been caused not because food wasn't available but because of bad governance—institutional failures that led to poor distribution of the available food, or even hoarding and storage in the face of starvation elsewhere. As Sen put it, "No substantial famine has ever occurred in any independent and democratic country with a relatively free press."

Should we let it rest there, then? Can we assume that the poor, though they may be eating little, do eat as much as they need to?

The world we live in today is for the most part too rich for the occasional lack of food to be a big part of the story of the persistence of poverty on a large scale.

The Consequences of Malnutrition

That also does not seem plausible. While Indians may prefer to buy things other than food as they get richer, they and their children are certainly not well nourished by any objective standard. Anemia is rampant; body mass indices are some of the lowest in the world; almost half of children under 5 are much too short for their age, and one-fifth are so skinny that they are considered to be "wasted."

And this is not without consequences. There is a lot of evidence that children suffering from malnutrition generally grow into less successful adults. In Kenya, children who were given deworming pills in school for two years went to school longer and earned, as young adults, 20 percent more than children in comparable schools who received deworming for just one year. Worms contribute to anemia and general malnutrition, essentially because they compete with the child for nutrients. And the negative impact of undernutrition starts before birth. In Tanzania, to cite just one example, children born to mothers who received sufficient amounts of iodine during pregnancy completed between one-third and one-half of a year more schooling than their siblings who were *in utero* when their mothers weren't being treated. It is a substantial increase, given that most of these children will complete only four or five years of schooling in total. In fact, the study concludes that if every mother took iodine capsules, there would be a 7.5 percent increase in the total educational attainment of children in central and southern Africa. This, in turn, could measurably affect lifetime productivity.

Better nutrition matters for adults, too. In another study, in Indonesia, researchers tested the effects of boosting people's intake of iron, a key nutrient that prevents anemia. They found that iron supplements made men able to work harder and significantly boosted income. A year's supply of iron-fortified fish sauce cost the equivalent of $6, and for a self-employed male, the yearly gain in earnings was nearly $40—an excellent investment.

If the gains are so obvious, why don't the poor eat better? Eating well doesn't have to be prohibitively expensive. Most mothers could surely afford iodized salt, which is now standard in many parts of the world, or one dose of iodine every two years (at 51 cents per dose). Poor households could easily get a lot more calories and other nutrients by spending less on expensive grains (like rice and wheat), sugar, and processed foods, and more on leafy vegetables and coarse grains. But in Kenya, when the NGO [nongovernmental organization] that was running the deworming program asked parents in some schools to pay a few cents for deworming their children, almost all refused, thus depriving their children of hundreds of dollars of extra earnings over their lifetime. . . .

The poor may well be more skeptical about supposed opportunities and the possibility of any radical change in their lives.

Spending Habits of the Poor

The poor often resist the wonderful plans we think up for them because they do not share our faith that those plans work, or work as well as we claim. We shouldn't forget, too, that other things may be more important in their lives than food. Poor people in the developing world spend large amounts on weddings, dowries, and christenings. Part of the reason is probably that they don't want to lose face, when the social custom is to spend a lot on those occasions. In South Africa, poor families often spend so lavishly on funerals that they skimp on food for months afterward.

And don't underestimate the power of factors like boredom. Life can be quite dull in a village. There is no movie theater, no concert hall. And not a lot of work, either. In rural Morocco, Oucha Mbarbk and his two neighbors told us they had worked about 70 days in agriculture and about 30 days in construction that year. Otherwise, they took care of their cattle and waited for jobs to materialize. All three men lived in small houses without water or sanitation. They struggled to find enough money to give their children a good education. But they each had a television, a parabolic antenna, a DVD player, and a cell phone. . . .

We often see the world of the poor as a land of missed opportunities and wonder why they don't invest in what would really make their lives better. But the poor may well be more skeptical about supposed opportunities and the possibility of any radical change in their lives. They often behave as if they think that any change that is significant enough to be worth sacrificing for will simply take too long. This could explain why they focus on the here and now, on living their lives as pleasantly as possible and celebrating when occasion demands it.

We asked Oucha Mbarbk what he would do if he had more money. He said he would buy more food. Then we asked him what he would do if he had even more money. He said he would buy better-tasting food. We were starting to feel very bad for him and his family, when we noticed the TV and other high-tech gadgets. Why had he bought all these things if he felt the family did not have enough to eat? He laughed, and said, "Oh, but television is more important than food!"

Periodical and Internet Sources Bibliography

The following articles have been selected to supplement the diverse views presented in this chapter.

David Callahan	"False Choices on Poverty," *American Prospect*, April 22, 2007.
Economist	"The Economics of Violence," April 14, 2011.
Jamie Holmes	"Why Can't More Poor People Escape Poverty?," *New Republic*, June 6, 2011.
International Trade Union Confederation (ITUC)	"A Recipe for Hunger: How the World Is Failing on Food," March 2009. www.ituc-csi.org.
Investor's Business Daily	"Poverty of Muslim World Can't Be Blamed on West," March 4, 2011.
Charles Kenny	"More People, Please," *Foreign Policy*, May 23, 2011.
Nicholas D. Kristof	"Pregnant (Again) and Poor," *New York Times*, April 4, 2009.
Barry Loberfeld	"What About the Poor?," *FrontPage Magazine*, August 13, 2008. www.frontpagemag.com.
Jonathan Owen	"Record Levels of Poverty Among Families with Wages," *Independent* (UK), December 5, 2010.
Robert Rector	"Marriage: America's Greatest Weapon Against Child Poverty," Heritage Foundation, September 16, 2010. www.heritage.org.
George Wehrfritz	"The Price of Survival," *Newsweek*, August 31, 2008.
Julia Whitty	"The Last Taboo," *Mother Jones*, May/June 2010.

GLOBALVIEWPOINTS

CHAPTER 4

Efforts to End Poverty

Foreign Aid in Africa Is Increasing Poverty

Dambisa Moyo

In the following viewpoint, Dambisa Moyo argues that foreign aid to Africa is doing more harm than good. Moyo claims that although short-term charity aid is sometimes warranted, long-term aid does not work to solve economic problems. Moyo contends that aid to Africa has resulted in rampant corruption in government, has prevented government from being answerable to the people, and has led to civil instability. Rather than supporting economic development, Moyo claims that aid puts Africans out of business and discourages investment. Moyo concludes that the current aid model of giving money for nothing needs to end. Moyo is an international economist and author of Dead Aid: Why Aid Is Not Working and How There Is a Better Way for Africa.

As you read, consider the following questions:

1. According to Moyo, over the past sixty years how much development-related aid has been transferred from rich countries to Africa?

2. What percentage of African public money comes from foreign aid, according to Moyo?

3. What alternative does the author suggest should replace the aid system that emphasizes handouts?

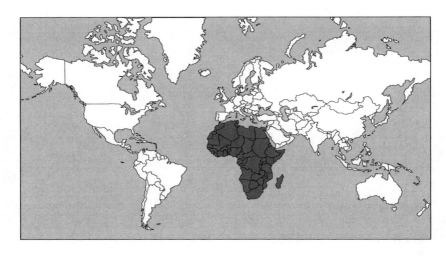

A month ago [February 2009] I visited Kibera, the largest slum in Africa. This suburb of Nairobi, the capital of Kenya, is home to more than one million people, who eke out a living in an area of about one square mile—roughly 75% the size of New York's Central Park. It is a sea of aluminum and cardboard shacks that forgotten families call home. The idea of a slum conjures up an image of children playing amidst piles of garbage, with no running water and the rank, rife stench of sewage. Kibera does not disappoint.

What is incredibly disappointing is the fact that just a few yards from Kibera stands the headquarters of the United Nations' agency for human settlements which, with an annual budget of millions of dollars, is mandated to "promote socially and environmentally sustainable towns and cities with the goal of providing adequate shelter for all." Kibera festers in Kenya, a country that has one of the highest ratios of development workers per capita. This is also the country where in 2004, British envoy Sir Edward Clay apologized for underestimating the scale of government corruption and failing to speak out earlier.

Aid to Africa

Giving alms to Africa remains one of the biggest ideas of our time—millions march for it, governments are judged by it, celebrities proselytize the need for it. Calls for more aid to Africa are growing louder, with advocates pushing for doubling the roughly $50 billion of international assistance that already goes to Africa each year.

Yet evidence overwhelmingly demonstrates that aid to Africa has made the poor poorer, and the growth slower. The insidious aid culture has left African countries more debt-laden, more inflation-prone, more vulnerable to the vagaries of the currency markets and more unattractive to higher-quality investment. It's increased the risk of civil conflict and unrest (the fact that over 60% of sub-Saharan Africa's population is under the age of 24 with few economic prospects is a cause for worry). Aid is an unmitigated political, economic and humanitarian disaster.

Evidence overwhelmingly demonstrates that aid to Africa has made the poor poorer, and the growth slower.

Few will deny that there is a clear moral imperative for humanitarian and charity-based aid to step in when necessary, such as during the 2004 tsunami in Asia. Nevertheless, it's worth reminding ourselves what emergency and charity-based aid can and cannot do. Aid-supported scholarships have certainly helped send African girls to school (never mind that they won't be able to find a job in their own countries once they have graduated). This kind of aid can provide Band-Aid solutions to alleviate immediate suffering, but by its very nature cannot be the platform for long-term sustainable growth.

Whatever its strengths and weaknesses, such charity-based aid is relatively small beer when compared to the sea of money that floods Africa each year in government-to-government aid or aid from large development institutions such as the World Bank.

Over the past 60 years at least $1 trillion of development-related aid has been transferred from rich countries to Africa. Yet real per capita income today is lower than it was in the 1970s, and more than 50% of the population—over 350 million people—live on less than a dollar a day, a figure that has nearly doubled in two decades.

Even after the very aggressive debt-relief campaigns in the 1990s, African countries still pay close to $20 billion in debt repayments per annum, a stark reminder that aid is not free. In order to keep the system going, debt is repaid at the expense of African education and health care. Well-meaning calls to cancel debt mean little when the cancellation is met with the fresh infusion of aid, and the vicious cycle starts up once again.

In 2005, just weeks ahead of a G8 [a group of eight major world economies] conference that had Africa at the top of its agenda, the International Monetary Fund [IMF] published a report entitled "Aid Will Not Lift Growth in Africa." The report cautioned that governments, donors and campaigners should be more modest in their claims that increased aid will solve Africa's problems. Despite such comments, no serious efforts have been made to wean Africa off this debilitating drug.

Aid and Corruption

The most obvious criticism of aid is its links to rampant corruption. Aid flows destined to help the average African end up supporting bloated bureaucracies in the form of the poor-country governments and donor-funded nongovernmental organizations. In a hearing before the U.S. Senate Committee on Foreign Relations in May 2004, Jeffrey Winters, a professor at Northwestern University, argued that the World Bank had participated in the corruption of roughly $100 billion of its loan funds intended for development.

As recently as 2002, the African Union, an organization of African nations, estimated that corruption was costing the continent $150 billion a year, as international donors were apparently turning a blind eye to the simple fact that aid money was inadvertently fueling graft. With few or no strings attached, it has been all too easy for the funds to be used for anything, save the developmental purpose for which they were intended.

In Zaire—known today as the Democratic Republic of the Congo—Irwin Blumenthal (whom the IMF had appointed to a post in the country's central bank) warned in 1978 that the system was so corrupt that there was "no (repeat, no) prospect for Zaire's creditors to get their money back." Still, the IMF soon gave the country the largest loan it had ever given an African nation. According to corruption watchdog agency Transparency International, Mobutu Sese Seko, Zaire's president from 1965 to 1997, is reputed to have stolen at least $5 billion from the country.

It's scarcely better today. A month ago, Malawi's former president Bakili Muluzi was charged with embezzling aid money worth $12 million. Zambia's former president Frederick Chiluba (a development darling during his 1991 to 2001 tenure) remains embroiled in a court case that has revealed millions of dollars frittered away from health, education and infrastructure toward his personal cash dispenser. Yet the aid keeps on coming.

A constant stream of "free" money is a perfect way to keep an inefficient or simply bad government in power.

Aid and Government

A nascent economy needs a transparent and accountable government and an efficient civil service to help meet social needs.

Its people need jobs and a belief in their country's future. A surfeit of aid has been shown to be unable to help achieve these goals.

A constant stream of "free" money is a perfect way to keep an inefficient or simply bad government in power. As aid flows in, there is nothing more for the government to do—it doesn't need to raise taxes, and as long as it pays the army, it doesn't have to take account of its disgruntled citizens. No matter that its citizens are disenfranchised (as with no taxation there can be no representation). All the government really needs to do is to court and cater to its foreign donors to stay in power.

Stuck in an aid world of no incentives, there is no reason for governments to seek other, better, more transparent ways of raising development finance (such as accessing the bond market, despite how hard that might be). The aid system encourages poor-country governments to pick up the phone and ask the donor agencies for the next capital infusion. It is no wonder that across Africa, over 70% of the public purse comes from foreign aid.

In Ethiopia, where aid constitutes more than 90% of the government budget, a mere 2% of the country's population has access to mobile phones. (The African country average is around 30%.) Might it not be preferable for the government to earn money by selling its mobile phone license, thereby generating much-needed development income and also providing its citizens with telephone service that could, in turn, spur economic activity?

Look what has happened in Ghana, a country where after decades of military rule brought about by a coup, a pro-market government has yielded encouraging developments. Farmers and fishermen now use mobile phones to communicate with their agents and customers across the country to find out where prices are most competitive. This translates into numerous opportunities for self-sustainability and income generation—which, with encouragement, could be easily replicated across the continent.

Aid and Business

To advance a country's economic prospects, governments need efficient civil service. But civil service is naturally prone to bureaucracy, and there is always the incipient danger of self-serving cronyism and the desire to bind citizens in endless, time-consuming red tape. What aid does is make that danger a grim reality. This helps to explain why doing business across much of Africa is a nightmare. In Cameroon, it takes a potential investor around 426 days to perform 15 procedures to gain a business license. What entrepreneur wants to spend 119 days filling out forms to start a business in Angola? He's much more likely to consider the U.S. (40 days and 19 procedures) or South Korea (17 days and 10 procedures).

Even what may appear as a benign intervention on the surface can have damning consequences. Say there is a mosquito-net maker in small-town Africa. Say he employs 10 people who together manufacture 500 nets a week. Typically, these 10 employees support upward of 15 relatives each. A Western government–inspired program generously supplies the affected region with 100,000 free mosquito nets. This promptly puts the mosquito-net manufacturer out of business, and now his 10 employees can no longer support their 150 dependents. In a couple of years, most of the donated nets will be torn and useless, but now there is no mosquito-net maker to go to. They'll have to get more aid. And African governments once again get to abdicate their responsibilities.

In a similar vein has been the approach to food aid, which historically has done little to support African farmers. Under the auspices of the U.S. Food for Peace program, each year millions of dollars are used to buy American-grown food that has to then be shipped across oceans. One wonders how a system of flooding foreign markets with American food, which

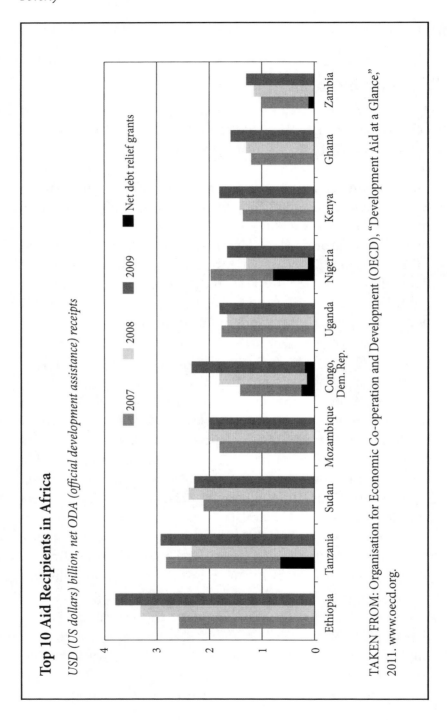

Top 10 Aid Recipients in Africa

USD (US dollars) billion, net ODA (official development assistance) receipts

TAKEN FROM: Organisation for Economic Co-operation and Development (OECD), "Development Aid at a Glance," 2011. www.oecd.org.

puts local farmers out of business, actually helps better Africa. A better strategy would be to use aid money to buy food from farmers within the country, and then distribute that food to the local citizens in need.

Even what may appear as a benign intervention on the surface can have damning consequences.

Then there is the issue of "Dutch disease," a term that describes how large inflows of money can kill off a country's export sector, by driving up home prices and thus making their goods too expensive for export. Aid has the same effect. Large dollar-denominated aid windfalls that envelop fragile developing economies cause the domestic currency to strengthen against foreign currencies. This is catastrophic for jobs in the poor country where people's livelihoods depend on being relatively competitive in the global market.

To fight aid-induced inflation, countries have to issue bonds to soak up the subsequent glut of money swamping the economy. In 2005, for example, Uganda was forced to issue such bonds to mop up excess liquidity to the tune of $700 million. The interest payments alone on this were a staggering $110 million, to be paid annually.

The stigma associated with countries relying on aid should also not be underestimated or ignored. It is the rare investor that wants to risk money in a country that is unable to stand on its own feet and manage its own affairs in a sustainable way.

Political Instability in Africa

Africa remains the most unstable continent in the world, beset by civil strife and war. Since 1996, 11 countries have been embroiled in civil wars. According to the Stockholm International Peace Research Institute, in the 1990s, Africa had more wars than the rest of the world combined. Although my country, Zambia, has not had the unfortunate experience of an outright civil war, growing up I experienced firsthand the discomfort of living under curfew (where everyone had to be in their homes between 6 p.m. and 6 a.m., which meant racing from work and school) and faced the fear of the uncertain outcomes of an attempted coup in 1991—sadly, experiences not uncommon to many Africans.

Civil clashes are often motivated by the knowledge that by seizing the seat of power, the victor gains virtually unfettered access to the package of aid that comes with it. In the last few months alone, there have been at least three political upheavals across the continent, in Mauritania, Guinea and Guinea-Bissau (each of which remains reliant on foreign aid). Madagascar's government was just overthrown in a coup this past week [in March 2009]. The ongoing political volatility across the continent serves as a reminder that aid-financed efforts to force-feed democracy to economies facing ever-growing poverty and difficult economic prospects remain, at best, precariously vulnerable. Long-term political success can only be achieved once a solid economic trajectory has been established.

Africa remains the most unstable continent in the world, beset by civil strife and war.

Proponents of aid are quick to argue that the $13 billion ($100 billion in today's terms) aid of the post–World War II Marshall Plan helped pull back a broken Europe from the brink of an economic abyss, and that aid could work, and would work, if Africa had a good policy environment.

The aid advocates skirt over the point that the Marshall Plan interventions were short, sharp and finite, unlike the open-ended commitments which imbue governments with a sense of entitlement rather than encouraging innovation. And aid supporters spend little time addressing the mystery of why a country in good working order would seek aid rather than other, better forms of financing. No country has ever achieved economic success by depending on aid to the degree that many African countries do.

An Alternative to Aid

The good news is we know what works; what delivers growth and reduces poverty. We know that economies that rely on open-ended commitments of aid almost universally fail, and those that do not depend on aid succeed. The latter is true for economically successful countries such as China and India, and even closer to home, in South Africa and Botswana. Their strategy of development finance emphasizes the important role of entrepreneurship and markets over a staid aid system of development that preaches handouts.

African countries could start by issuing bonds to raise cash. To be sure, the traditional capital markets of the U.S. and Europe remain challenging. However, African countries could explore opportunities to raise capital in more nontraditional markets such as the Middle East and China (whose foreign exchange reserves are more than $4 trillion). Moreover, the current market malaise provides an opening for African countries to focus on acquiring credit ratings (a prerequisite to accessing the bond markets), and preparing themselves for the time when the capital markets return to some semblance of normalcy.

Governments need to attract more foreign direct investment by creating attractive tax structures and reducing the red tape and complex regulations for businesses. African nations should also focus on increasing trade; China is one promising partner. And Western countries can help by cutting off the cycle of giving something for nothing. It's time for a change.

Foreign Aid in Africa Is Helping to Fight Poverty

Kevin Watkins

In the following viewpoint, Kevin Watkins argues against Dambisa Moyo's proposal to end foreign aid to Africa. Watkins denies that aid increases poverty, claiming that there is evidence that aid has resulted in economic growth in Africa. Furthermore, Watkins claims that although aid to Africa in the 1980s and 1990s was not an overall success story, it has been working well since the beginning of the century to improve education and health. He concludes that the current focus should be on improving the effectiveness of aid to Africa, not on discontinuing aid. Watkins is senior visiting research fellow at the Global Economic Governance Programme at University College of the University of Oxford in England.

As you read, consider the following questions:

1. According to Watkins, what fraction of Africa's population lives in extreme poverty?

2. The author contends that before the global economic crisis, how many non–oil exporting countries in Africa were growing at more than 5 percent a year?

3. Rather than cutting aid, Watkins suggests that the real debate should be about how to do what?

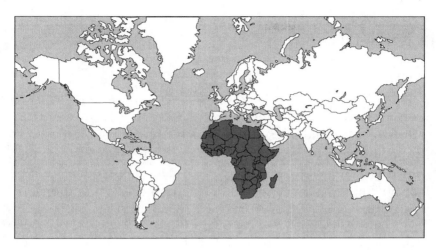

In March [2009], thousands of campaigners from development charities took to the streets of London. Their target was the G-20 summit [a meeting of finance ministers and central bank governors from around the world]. With the global economic downturn pushing Africa into recession, the marchers had a simple message for the governments of rich countries. As one banner put it: "Remember Africa—increase aid to fight poverty."

An Argument Against Aid

If you believe Dambisa Moyo, a Zambian economist who worked at Goldman Sachs, the campaigners should have stayed at home. In *Dead Aid[: Why Aid Is Not Working and How There Is a Better Way for Africa]*, she argues that development assistance is not merely a waste of money, but that [it] is a cause of Africa's persistent poverty. Rejecting what she describes as "orchestrated worldwide pity," Moyo also has a simple but stark message: "Aid has been, and continues to be, an unmitigated political, economic, and humanitarian disaster." She is leading a crusade to cut development assistance—and she can point to an impressive fan base. Writing in the foreword, the historian Niall Ferguson tells us that he "was left wanting a lot more Moyo, and a lot less Bono [lead singer of the band U2 and outspoken activist]." So what is Moyo's appeal?

Her starting point is that aid is not working. The line of argument runs roughly as follows. Over the last few decades, donors have pumped billions of dollars in aid into Africa. Meanwhile, the number of poor people in the region has continued to rise. Why has so much aid done so little good? Moyo provides a statistical and anecdotal bombardment aimed at showing that aid chokes off economic growth, sponsors corruption, and fosters financial dependence on foreign donors. Why bother with taxing your citizens when you have access to easy money in the form of aid?

Moyo's solution to the aid problem is nothing if not clear-cut. She advocates a hefty dose of cold turkey. "What if," she asks, "African countries each received a phone call . . . telling them that in exactly five years the aid taps would be shut off—permanently?"

As good fortune would have it, Moyo has a ready-made antidote for aid dependence. African governments, she argues, should raise money by issuing bonds on international credit markets. *Dead Aid* also offers some wider advice on economic growth. Instead of obsessing over more aid, we are told, Africa should be calling for fairer trade and stepping up efforts to attract Chinese investment. And civil society organisations should worry less about democracy because "it matters little to a starving African family whether they can vote or not."

What should we make of all this? Is it time for Bono and [British singer and political activist] Bob Geldof to stop haranguing rich world leaders for a better deal for Africa? Should Oxfam [International] campaigners be marching under the banner "Turn Off the Aid Taps Now"?

Aid and Poverty

These questions matter. Half of Africa's population—some 390m people—live in extreme poverty. Almost 5m children do not live to see their fifth birthday because of diseases like malaria, diarrhoea, and HIV/AIDS. And in an increasingly knowledge-based global economy, one in three primary school-age kids are out of school. Fighting this deprivation is an ethical and humanitarian imperative. Aid is supposed to be a weapon in this fight, not an iron cage for keeping the poor where they are.

The problem with *Dead Aid* is that it does nothing to advance the debate on development assistance. This is partly because the author is bent on tilting at windmills. Most advocates for increased development assistance recognise that aid is not a cure-all for poverty and that trade is critically important (most of Moyo's evidence on trade is actually lifted from Oxfam). They also recognise that corruption is a serious problem, that aid is often less effective than it should be, and that aid flows have to be managed to prevent economic distortions that can harm growth prospects. Compared with Moyo, Bob Geldof is a model of nuance and cautious realism.

Moyo's solution to the aid problem is nothing if not clear-cut. She advocates a hefty dose of cold turkey.

The more serious difficulty with *Dead Aid* is the evidence base. Take the argument three decades of aid have served only to increase poverty and reduce economic growth. In fact, there is a large body of academic work pointing in the opposite direction: On average, aid tends to raise growth levels. Establishing causality from aid to growth, or vice versa, is inherently difficult. But Moyo is apparently oblivious to the causality problem. Using her logic, you could argue that fire engines cause fires because you find them near burning houses.

The difficulties don't end there. Thirty years ago, much of what passed as aid was directed not towards African growth and poverty reduction, but to Cold War priorities. Why would you expect aid replenishments to the Swiss bank accounts of Daniel Arap Moi [president of Kenya from 1978–2002] or Mobutu Sese Seko [president of Zaire from 1965–1997] to help Africa's poor?

Since 2000, for the first time in over three decades, the incidence of poverty in Africa has been falling.

The Impact of Past Aid

One of the most disconcerting aspects of *Dead Aid* is its failure to explore why past aid has delivered so little. The impact of the debt crisis in undermining economic growth, reinforcing poverty, and eroding health and education systems is ignored. Structural adjustment programmes which made aid conditional on governments signing up for stringent deflation and damaging experiments in 'big-bang' market liberalisation barely get a mention. This is despite the fact that Moyo's home country, Zambia, was one of the worst affected countries, with the agricultural sector left devastated by a botched liberalisation of food marketing.

Whatever the factors behind the failures of the 1980s and 1990s, recent evidence points in a more positive direction. Before the economic crisis struck, eighteen non–oil exporting economies in Africa—from Burkina Faso and Mali to Ghana, Tanzania and Mozambique—were growing at more than 5 per cent a year. For the record, all of these countries are highly aid-dependent. Higher growth has brought with it some fragile gains in poverty reduction. Since 2000, for the first time in over three decades, the incidence of poverty in Africa has been falling—from 58 per cent to 51 per cent. Moyo turns a blind eye to evidence for an obvious reason: It doesn't back her prejudices.

It's not just the economic growth and poverty story that Moyo misrepresents. Throughout the book, Africa is repre-

The Solution to Aid Abuse

The solution to aid abuse is the fight for accountability and transparency to make it serve its purpose, not to cut off aid. And when aid is perverted by donor countries to promote business interests or to buy the loyalty of corrupt regimes for geopolitical ends, this is not aid: It is economic and political corruption.

Dereje Alemayehu and Donu Kogbara,
"Should Foreign Investment Replace Aid in Africa?,"
New Internationalist, *no. 445, September 2011.*

sented as a basket case for human development—"zero-progress" zone for the targets set under the Millennium Development Goals (MDGs). This is a caricature.

Consider first the record on education. Since 2000, the primary school enrolment rates have been growing at six times the rate of the 1990s. In Tanzania, to take one example, aid finance has supported policies that include the removal of school fees, classroom construction in remote areas, and the provision of textbooks. The result: another 3 million kids in school. Countries such as Senegal and Zambia have made dramatic progress in cutting out-of-school numbers, with aid finance playing an important role.

In the health sector, international aid initiatives are saving lives. Today, there are just over two million HIV/AIDS sufferers in Africa receiving antiretroviral drugs. Six years ago that figure was 50,000. Childhood deaths from malaria have also fallen sharply in countries such as Ethiopia, Rwanda and Tanzania, thanks in part to a rapid scaling-up of insecticide-treated bed net provision and anti-malarial drugs.

The Need to Increase Aid Effectiveness

None of this is to suggest that aid is an unmitigated success story. It patently is not. But to suggest that shock therapy aid cuts are the answer is unwarranted and frankly irresponsible. Try telling a mother whose kid is sleeping under an anti-malarial bed net, or has just got a chance to go to school, that cold turkey is the best option.

The real debate should be over how to increase aid effectiveness. Aid works best when governments put in place sensible economic policies, effective strategies for poverty reduction, budget transparency and measures for tackling corruption. Many African governments fail these tests with impunity, partly because they lack accountability to their citizens. That's why Moyo is wrong to argue for democracy to be put on the back burner. But not all of these problems can be laid at the door of aid recipients. As Michela Wrong demonstrates in her extraordinary book on Kenya, *It's Our Turn to Eat*, it takes two to tango on corruption—and northern governments (including Britain) are often complicit.

To suggest that shock therapy aid cuts are the answer is unwarranted and frankly irresponsible.

When it comes to aid effectiveness, donors have a mixed record. In their public statements, they repeatedly stress their collective commitment to improve coordination, work through national reporting systems, and support nationally owned plans. These things matter. When donors fail to coordinate or use national systems, the transaction costs of aid go up, and the benefits go down. Yet too often, donors continue to create parallel aid structures and to duplicate their efforts. Does Niger really need over 600 separate donor missions each year? And for all the talk of national ownership, aid provided through the IMF [International Monetary Fund] continues to come with more strings attached than your average marionette.

In one respect, Moyo is a victim of bad timing. Before the financial crisis, a few African governments were starting to raise money on international bond markets. These markets were never going to replace aid. But the global credit collapse has now firmly closed the door to bond markets for Africa. It has also served to underline the lesson that African governments, like all governments, should think twice about taking advice from international investment banks.

In the last analysis, Africa's future does not depend on aid. It depends on its people and its governments. Yet aid can make a difference. At a time when the future of millions of people in Africa is threatened by a crisis the region played no part in creating, human solidarity and social justice demand that we call on rich-country governments to increase aid—and to act now.

More Moyo and a lot less Bono? Thanks, but no thanks.

Global Redistribution of Incomes Is a Solution to Inequality and Poverty

Claire Melamed

In the following viewpoint, Claire Melamed argues that global income inequality needs to be addressed through the redistribution of incomes on a global level. Although foreign aid is one such mechanism to redistribute incomes globally, Melamed claims that is not the best method and that it has several problems. Melamed contends that renewed interest in social protection and tax reform is creating an opportunity for income redistribution. She justifies global redistribution of incomes by pointing to the ways in which inequality is created, and she concludes that redistribution would have many positive effects worldwide. Melamed is the head of the Growth, Poverty and Inequality Programme at the Overseas Development Institute in London.

As you read, consider the following questions:

1. According to Melamed, the United Kingdom and the United States both spend what percentage of their respective budgets on national welfare?
2. Wealth is currently redistributed from poor to rich by what two mechanisms, according to the author?

Claire Melamed, "Global Redistribution as a Solution to Poverty," *IDS In Focus Policy Briefing*, vol. 11, no. 1, October 2009, pp. 1–3. Copyright © 2009 by The Institute of Development Studies. All rights reserved. Reproduced by permission.

3. According to Melamed, how much money is taken from developing countries each year by multinational companies who evade taxes?

The scale of global inequality is universally agreed to be unacceptable. Yet little has been done to tackle inequality directly through redistribution of incomes on a global level. Although redistribution, through tax and welfare systems, is at the heart of antipoverty programmes in developed countries, it has not been a serious proposition at an international level until now. The financial crisis has propelled two interventions onto the agenda which together look like a global welfare state: social protection and tax reform. This [viewpoint] asks, What is driving global inequality? And how can redistribution help tackle existing inequalities and contribute to poverty reduction internationally?

Global Income Inequality

The scale of global inequalities in income and wealth has been described as 'extraordinary', 'incredible' and 'obscene' by Oxfam [International], [British prime minister] David Cameron and [former South African president] Nelson Mandela respectively. Most people seem to agree. Certainly, no one could argue that a world where, according to the United Nations Human Development Report, the richest 500 people earn more than the poorest 416 million is anything other than remarkable.

But until now very little effort has been expended on addressing income inequality directly through redistribution of incomes on a global level. It has been assumed that any redistribution should be primarily at the national level, and that any welfare or social protection schemes funded through redistributive taxation will be limited to what national governments can afford.

The financial crisis may have changed that. It has created problems that are beyond the capacity of individual governments to solve, reigniting interest in a broader range of global policies and actions. It has also pushed new issues up the agenda—chiefly social protection and tax reform—issues that are at the heart of tackling poverty at a national level in many countries, and could potentially form the pillars of a global welfare system.

Given the near-universal consensus that inequality is a bad thing, it is surprising that so little attention has been given to policies to directly tackle it, as a way of reducing poverty.

This [viewpoint] asks the critical question: Can a global model of poverty reduction through redistribution from rich to poor work? And if so, how?

Given the near-universal consensus that inequality is a bad thing, it is surprising that so little attention has been given to policies to directly tackle it, as a way of reducing poverty. Despite the efforts of a few, such as Branko Milanovic at the World Bank, who has suggested a 'commodities tax' as a way of redistributing incomes worldwide, and Kevin Watkins at UNESCO [United Nations Educational, Scientific and Cultural Organization], who has suggested that reducing inequality becomes an explicit international objective in any new agreement taking forward the Millennium Development Goals, redistributing incomes as a way of reducing poverty is almost absent from the international agenda.

This is all the more striking since redistribution, through tax and welfare systems, is at the heart of antipoverty programmes in donor countries. The UK [United Kingdom] and the US [United States] both spend around 60 per cent of the central government budget on welfare—money that comes from taxing the better off and that is spent largely on cash transfers, housing, and providing medical care for the poor. The modest level of redistribution involved has not prevented growing inequalities in these countries, but it has ensured a floor below which the majority of the population (subject to certain exclusions, such as asylum seekers) are not allowed to fall.

It's time to take seriously the possibilities for global redistribution of incomes as a mechanism to end poverty.

International Redistribution Through Aid

The closest thing to tax and spend in international development is aid. Money from taxpayers in rich countries is spent through governments or other agencies on (some) poor people in (some) poor countries. But this falls short of an international redistributive mechanism for many reasons:

1. *Aid is highly conditional.* The most significant conditionality is the political circumstances of the donor country. Aid levels fall or rise not because of need in poor countries, but because of political calculations in rich countries.

2. *Many countries do not direct aid to where people are poorest.* According to the OECD's [Organisation for Economic Co-operation and Development's] figures, less than a third of US international aid is spent in the poorest countries. The UK is one of the few countries where poverty reduction is an explicit and legally binding objective of aid spending. Too often aid is spent in countries that are politically expedient, rather than where the need is greatest.

3. *Even if aid reaches the poorest countries, there is no guarantee that it will be spent on the poorest people.* The precipitous falls in aid to agriculture over the last 20 years, despite the fact that most of the world's poorest live in rural areas, illustrates that national governments, as well as donors, will not necessarily spend aid in a redistributive manner.

Rather than redistribution, it is growth that is assumed to be the main engine of poverty reduction. But even at the high average rates of growth seen in many developing countries before the financial crisis, poverty reduction is a slow business if we rely on growth alone. Many countries are not on track to achieve the Millennium Development Goal of halving world poverty by 2015. And since the food and finance crises of 2008, and their disastrous impact on global growth rates, that goal is even more distant. Government efforts to increase both the rate of growth and the extent to which poor people feel the benefits of that growth are important. But growth is not the end of the story.

It's time to take seriously the possibilities for global redistribution of incomes as a mechanism to end poverty. Given the increasingly global nature of economic relationships, it seems illogical and unfair to insist that the redistribution of the benefits of globally managed economic activity should be defined by national boundaries.

The Drivers of Inequality

Inequality doesn't happen by accident—it is created at both national and international levels by the combined workings of politics, of social and gender norms, and by the actions of individual companies and people. Politics and business work together to redistribute wealth globally from poor to rich, and as many governments have found to their cost, reversing that flow involves taking on the most powerful interests both globally and nationally.

As governments compete for investment on the basis of cheap labour, they also become complicit in driving increases in inequality. For instance, police are employed in Bangladesh to subdue women garment workers striking to demand a bigger percentage of the profits be given to them in wages. But the same government suspends labour laws in so-called 'export processing zones' to allow companies to extract an even higher rate of profit from their operations. The result? Value is transferred from Bangladeshi workers to company owners in Bangladesh, and via supply chains to the owners of retail companies in the US and Europe.

Similarly, competition for scarce investment capital on the basis of low taxes is increasing levels of inequity in mineral-rich countries of Africa. Global mining companies are taking advantage of generous tax breaks to extract the natural resource wealth that sits in the ground and take it out of the country. This leads to huge profits for the companies and almost no revenue for either governments or workers in the countries where the resources originate.

The combined effect of governments basing policy on what is good for business, and companies responding enthusiastically to the new opportunities created, is the rising levels of inequality that we see in the world today.

It also represents a huge missed opportunity for poverty reduction. An estimated 160 million dollars is exacted from developing countries through tax evasion by multinational companies every year. If even a fraction of that money was spent on health services, or on cash transfers, the results could be dramatic.

Ideas for Curbing Inequality

Now could be the moment to challenge the international coyness about redistributing incomes. The financial crisis has created a small gap in the political firmament in which global redistribution could fit.

Social protection is clearly an idea whose time has come. The combined effect of the food and financial crises is reversing development gains in many countries, and the scale of human need is forcing a response. The communiqué of the G-20 leaders [a group of finance ministers and central bank governors from around the world] meeting in London in April [2009] contained two references to social protection, and a

Wealth Levels Around the World

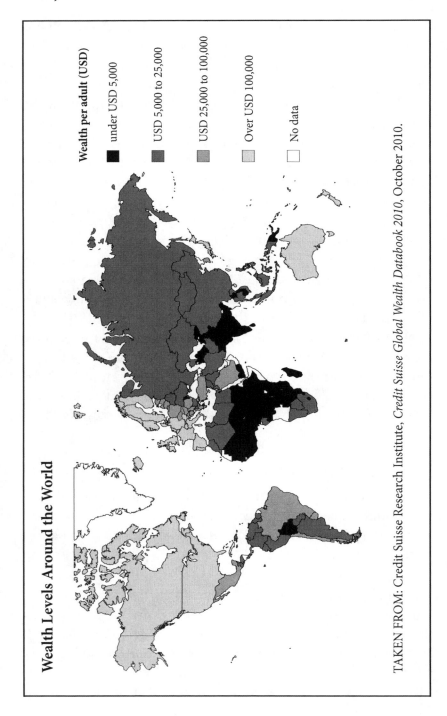

Wealth per adult (USD)

■ under USD 5,000

▨ USD 5,000 to 25,000

▨ USD 25,000 to 100,000

▢ Over USD 100,000

□ No data

TAKEN FROM: Credit Suisse Research Institute, *Credit Suisse Global Wealth Databook 2010*, October 2010.

commitment to provide resources for it. The African Union's recently agreed 'social policy framework' contains a commitment to invest in social protection on the continent.

But, globally, the ambitions for social protection will quickly fall short unless it is adequately funded. This is where some of the other proposals that have seen new life since the financial crisis come in.

We might be astonished at what a modest redistribution of incomes could achieve.

The renewed interest in tax as a source of funding for development opens up the possibility of curbing at least some of the transfer of wealth from poor to rich, and creating something akin to a global progressive tax system. The financial crisis has helped by creating incentives for all countries, rich and poor, to get tough on tax evasion and financial transparency. Other ideas are back on the table too, such as a currency transaction tax which could redistribute income from financial institutions to poor people via a central administrative organisation.

These all tackle redistribution after the event—once inequalities already exist, tax and welfare systems can redress the balance very slightly. It can only be a part of an equity agenda that also has to encompass proposals to make growth happen in a way that generates fewer inequalities. But we might be astonished at what a modest redistribution of incomes could achieve.

The Benefits of Redistribution

If redistributed incomes were spent on providing cash transfers to people unable to work, and if those in work were guaranteed a minimum wage, and if governments guaranteed free health, sanitation and education services for everyone, this could free up an enormous amount of time and energy that currently people are expending simply to survive.

People working seven rather than fifteen hours to earn the money they need to survive and to support elderly or ill relatives would suddenly have the time to educate themselves, to play with their children, or to take part in community organising. The result? Better skills, happier families or better-resourced communities. Women freed from the four-hour daily grind of collecting water could start businesses, participate in local decision making, or simply lead happier and more relaxed lives.

A robust redistributive system would also prevent the kind of reversals in progress on development that have been caused by the recent food and financial crises. Progress on development has been shown to be more fragile than perhaps was realised, with many tens of millions of people now predicted to be plunged back into poverty as a result of these joint shocks. A global system to redistribute incomes and provide a guaranteed standard of living for all would limit the terrible human cost of shocks, and protect poor people from bearing the brunt of global disasters.

Rapid Growth, Even with Inequality, Is the Best Way to Fight Poverty

Arvind Panagariya

In the following viewpoint, Arvind Panagariya argues that swift and continuous economic growth is the only way to make a serious dent in poverty in individual countries. Panagariya claims that growth not only directly reduces the poverty of individuals but also creates revenue for national programs aiming to reduce poverty. Panagariya admits that growth creates inequality but denies that this is a problem. As long as inequality does not result in abject poverty, he concludes that inequality is tolerable and works to motivate further growth. Panagariya is the Jagdish Bhagwati Professor of Indian Political Economy at Columbia University and author of India: The Emerging Giant.

As you read, consider the following questions:

1. According to Panagariya, why were India's antipoverty programs grossly underfunded for decades?
2. What two examples of measuring inequality does the author give?
3. What analogy does Panagariya use to support his view that inequality is tolerable in a growing economy?

Arvind Panagariya, "Growing Out of Poverty," *Finance & Development*, vol. 47, no. 3, September 2010, pp. 22–23. Copyright © 2010 by the International Monetary Fund. All rights reserved. Reproduced by permission.

There can be little hope of making a major dent in poverty in low-income countries—many of them in South Asia and Africa—without sustained rapid growth. Rapid growth provides gainful employment to many while generating swiftly rising tax revenues to finance antipoverty programs. Critics assert that growth barely trickles down to the poor, ignoring the reality that without it, low-income countries would lack fiscal resources for redistribution on a sustained basis.

The Impact of Growth on Poverty

Poverty alleviation has been a top priority for Indian leaders since the launch of the country's development program in 1950. Yet, for decades, India's antipoverty programs were grossly underfunded because the country was poor and grew very slowly. That low income and slow growth denied the country's poor both the direct benefits of growth—increased employment opportunities—and the indirect benefit—well-funded antipoverty programs. In contrast, countries such as the Republic of Korea and Taiwan Province of China, which managed to launch their economies into high-growth orbits in the early 1960s, quickly pulled their entire populations out of poverty. More recently, China has moved in the same direction.

In India, it was the accumulation of slow growth for three decades followed by some acceleration that finally began to make a dent in poverty. But it was only after another two to three decades of approximately 6 percent annual growth that the country could afford to introduce large-scale social programs, such as the employment guarantee scheme for rural households and effective rights to education and food security. That these programs remain poorly conceived with possible adverse consequences for growth is, of course, another matter.

While growth is crucial to generating the resources needed to finance large-scale antipoverty programs, its direct contribution to poverty alleviation should not be underestimated either. In the Republic of Korea and Taiwan Province of China in the 1960s and more recently in China and Vietnam, rapid growth of labor-intensive industry pulled large proportions of agricultural workers into well-paid manufacturing jobs. For example, 9.4 percent of the Korean workforce was employed in industry in 1965, compared with 21.6 percent in 1980, while agricultural employment fell from 58.6 percent to 34 percent over the same period. Reflecting rising productivity, average real wages rose at an annual rate exceeding 10 percent during this period.

Symmetrically, the poor are helped less when policies hinder the growth of labor-intensive industry. For a long time, India limited the production of virtually all labor-intensive products, such as apparel, footwear, toys, and light consumer goods, to enterprises with an investment ceiling of approximately $100,000 (later revised to $250,000). This resulted in the proliferation of highly inefficient tiny enterprises with limited ability to exploit the vast world markets in labor-intensive products. Indian toys never made it into the world markets, and the country's share in the U.S. apparel market today is about the same as that of much smaller Bangladesh. Although this practice has been virtually eliminated, stringent labor laws in the formal sector still inhibit the entry of large-scale manufacturing firms in the labor-intensive industries. Growth in India has been led by capital- and skilled-labor-intensive sectors, such as automobiles, auto parts, petroleum refining, steel, information technology, and pharmaceuticals. The result has been an extremely slow shift of India's workforce from agriculture to industry and, therefore, a failure to exploit fully the potential direct impact of growth on poverty reduction. This has naturally placed a greater burden on antipoverty programs. Unfortunately, these programs require the poor to stay where they are to receive benefits, which inhibits migration out of low-productivity employment such as agriculture.

Growth and Increased Inequality

When confronted with the evidence that no country has been able to cut poverty drastically without growth, critics shift the debate to inequality. They argue that even if growth helps reduce poverty, it should be moderated so that it does not increase inequality. It is harder to pin down the critics when it comes to inequality, because there are many alternative measures of it and they need not move in the same direction.

For example, we could look at the relationship of growth to the overall distribution of income across the national population as measured by the Gini coefficient (which ranges from 0 for total equality of income distribution to 1 for total inequality). Alternatively, we could worry about the average income of the top 5 percent of the population relative to the bottom 5 percent. It is possible—indeed, likely under plausible conditions—that even as the former measure shows declining inequality, the latter exhibits the opposite.

When confronted with the evidence that no country has been able to cut poverty drastically without growth, critics shift the debate to inequality.

Inequality can also be measured in terms of the differences between average urban and rural incomes. We could also be concerned about regional inequality as measured by the differences in per capita incomes across states. Then there is wage inequality between skilled and unskilled workers, and between workers in the formal and informal sectors. The list goes on.

There are good reasons why inequality according to some of these measures would be rising with growth. For example, the ratio of the income of the top 5 percent to the bottom 5 percent of individuals is almost certain to increase in a rapidly growing economy. For sustained rapid growth to occur, a handful of entrepreneurs must create a lot of wealth through legitimate means. These entrepreneurs are bound to end up with a significant proportion of that wealth. After all, it is the prospect of keeping a significant share of the wealth they create that motivates individuals to create wealth in the first place. Similarly, in the early stages of growth, rapid growth often concentrates in a few urban enclaves, which may increase urban-rural as well as regional inequality.

The Importance of Relative Wealth

Therefore, the real question is not whether rapid growth increases inequality, but whether the form of inequality that citizens find offensive is rising and, if so, what to do about it. Inequality that results in abject poverty for a portion of the population is reprehensible, and the fight against it must take precedence. As long as abject poverty exists, the largest gains in fighting the most offensive forms of inequality are likely to accrue from poverty alleviation. For instance, because the poor are concentrated in rural areas, raising rural incomes through antipoverty programs and also through worker migration to urban areas would automatically reduce urban-rural inequality. The poor also tend to be concentrated in particular regions, so concentrating antipoverty programs in those regions will alleviate regional inequality.

Ironically, the measure of inequality on which economists most commonly focus—the Gini coefficient calculated for the entire nation or a specific region—has perhaps the least relevance to an individual citizen's perception of his or her welfare. Try asking a villager whether he knows the direction of movement of the Gini coefficient in his state or country in the previous 10 years, or whether the 10 percent increase in the national or provincial Gini in the past 10 years bothers him. You can be sure that he will not understand the question. On the other hand, as I learned on a recent visit to my ancestral village, the villager will be concerned about why the incomes in his village have not risen as rapidly as those in the city next door. When it comes to inequality, individuals evaluate themselves within their immediate context, often limited to their neighbors, friends, coworkers, and nearby municipalities.

There are two final points:

- First, inequality is certainly more tolerable in a growing economy. When everyone is moving up on an escalator, the fact that some manage to walk or run up on it is less bothersome than if the escalator is stuck, leaving some with no hope of reaching the top.

- Second, if wealth accumulation through legitimate means takes place in an open and competitive environment, inequality can have an inspirational effect. In 1997, when [Microsoft chairman] Bill Gates—who had become a multibillionaire within a matter of years—first visited India, he inspired awe among young Indians. But 10 years later, in 2007, when *Forbes* magazine reported as many as 54 billionaires within India, many among the young said to themselves: They are no different than me—if they can do it, I can do it!

If wealth accumulation through legitimate means takes place in an open and competitive environment, inequality can have an inspirational effect.

Azim Premji—chairman of the information technology multinational Wipro and a self-made billionaire who maintains a modest lifestyle, flying economy class and driving a Toyota—put it this way to a British Broadcasting Corporation correspondent in 2007: "With the attention I got on my wealth, I thought I would have become a source of resentment, but it is just the other way around—it just generates that much more ambition in many people."

This same inspirational impact also works at the collective level. When Korea, China, and Taiwan Province of China grew rapidly, politicians in India would say, "We cannot do what they do; they are Chinese and we are Indians!" When the Indian regions of Haryana, Maharashtra, and Gujarat grew similarly rapidly, politicians in Bihar and Orissa could no longer make the same excuse. Instead, they were obliged to rethink policies in their states.

Less than five years ago, the Indian press was filled with warnings of impending revolution due to rising regional inequalities. Today, the same space is filled with the stories of how the chief ministers of Bihar and Orissa have turned their states around, delivering growth rates of 8 to 9 percent.

Removing Barriers to Trade Would Help Decrease Poverty

William Easterly

In the following viewpoint, William Easterly argues that trade-fueled growth through private business is the only way to eliminate poverty. Easterly contends that the international community has not given sufficient priority to the importance of trade in the Millennium Development Goals. In particular, Easterly claims that violations of free trade are rampant, with the United States and the European Union utilizing quotas and subsidies that harm farmers in poor countries. Easterly concludes that without resolving these trade distortions, eliminating poverty will be impossible. Easterly is professor of economics at New York University and codirector of its Development Research Institute.

As you read, consider the following questions:

1. According to Easterly, which of the Millennium Development Goals has been ignored?

2. The author claims that US cotton subsidies do what to export prices?

3. The author insinuates that what types of policies are preferable to foreign aid?

The Millennium Development Goals [MDGs] tragically misused the world's goodwill to support failed official aid approaches to global poverty and gave virtually no support to proven approaches. Economists such as Jeffrey Sachs might argue that the system can be improved by ditching bilateral aid and moving towards a "multi-donor" approach modeled on the Global Fund to Fight AIDS, Tuberculosis and Malaria. But current experience and history both speak loudly that the only real engine of growth out of poverty is private business, and there is no evidence that aid fuels such growth.

Of the eight [MDG] goals, only the eighth faintly recognises private business, through its call for a "non-discriminatory trading system". This anodyne language refers to the scandal of rich countries perpetuating barriers that favour a tiny number of their businesses at the expense of impoverished millions elsewhere. Yet the trade MDG received virtually no attention from the wider campaign, has seen no action, and even its failure has received virtually no attention in the current [September 2010] MDG summit hoopla.

Barriers to Effective Trade

This is all the more misguided because trade-fuelled growth not only decreases poverty, but also indirectly helps all the other MDGs. Yet in the US alone, the violations of the trade goal are legion. US consumers have long paid about twice the world price for sugar because of import quotas protecting about 9,000 domestic sugar producers. The European Union is similarly guilty.

Equally egregious subsidies are handed out to US cotton producers, which flood the world market, depressing export prices. These hit the lowest-cost cotton producers in the global economy, which also happen to be some of the poorest nations on earth: Mali, Burkina Faso and Chad.

According to an Oxfam [International] study, eliminating US cotton subsidies would "improve the welfare of over one

---

The Benefits of International Trade

A core element of globalization is the expansion of world trade through the elimination or reduction of trade barriers, such as import tariffs. Greater imports offer consumers a wider variety of goods at lower prices, while providing strong incentives for domestic industries to remain competitive. Exports, often a source of economic growth for developing nations, stimulate job creation as industries sell beyond their borders. More generally, trade enhances national competitiveness by driving workers to focus on those vocations where they, and their country, have a competitive advantage. Trade promotes economic resilience and flexibility, as higher imports help to offset adverse domestic supply shocks. Greater openness can also stimulate foreign investment, which would be a source of employment for the local workforce and could bring along new technologies—thus promoting higher productivity.

International Monetary Fund,
"Globalization: A Brief Overview,"
Issues Brief, no. 08/02, May 2008.

---

million West African households—10 million people—by increasing their incomes from cotton by 8 to 20 per cent".

Brahima Outtara, a small cotton farmer in Logokourani, Burkina Faso, described the status quo to the aid agency a few years ago: "Cotton prices are too low to keep our children in school, or to buy food and pay for health."

To be fair, the US government has occasionally tried to promote trade with poor countries, such as under the African Growth and Opportunity Act [AGOA], a bipartisan effort over the last three presidents to admit African exports duty free. Sadly, however, even this demonstrates the indifference of US trade policy towards the poor.

The biggest success story was textile exports from Madagascar to the US—but the US kicked Madagascar out of the AGOA at Christmas 2009. The excuse for this tragic debacle was that Madagascar was failing to make progress on democracy; an odd excuse given the continued AGOA eligibility of Cameroon, where the dictator Paul Biya has been in power for 28 violent years. Angola, Chad and even the Democratic Republic of the Congo are also still in. The Madagascan textile industry, meanwhile, has collapsed.

The Silence on Trade

In spite of all this, the great advocacy campaign for the millennium goals still ignores private business growth from trade, with a few occasional exceptions such as Oxfam. The burst of advocacy in 2005 surrounding the Group of Eight [G8, a group of eight major economies] summit and the Live 8 concerts scored a success on the G8 increasing aid, but nothing on trade.

The UN [United Nations] has continuously engaged US private business on virtually every poverty-reducing MDG except the one on trade that would reduce poverty-increasing subsidies to US private business. And while the UN will hold a "private sector forum" on September 22 as part of the MDG summit, the website for this forum makes no mention of rich-country trade protection.

The great advocacy campaign for the millennium goals still ignores private business growth from trade, with a few occasional exceptions.

The US government, for its part, announced recently its "strategy to meet the Millennium Development Goals". The proportion of this report devoted to the US government's own subsidies, quotas and tariffs affecting the poor is: zero. News coverage reflects all this—using Google News to search among thousands of articles on the millennium goals over the past week, the number that mention, say, "cotton subsidies" or "sugar quotas" is so far: zero.

It is already clear that the goals will not be met by their target date of 2015. One can already predict that the ruckus accompanying this failure will be loud about aid, but mostly silent about trade. It will also be loud about the failure of state actions to promote development, but mostly silent about the lost opportunities to allow poor countries' efficient private businesspeople to lift themselves out of poverty.

Globalization Is Not Clearly the Cause of Reduced Poverty or Increased Inequality

Pranab Bardhan

In the following viewpoint, Pranab Bardhan argues that globalization is improperly credited as the cause of both increased economic inequality and reduced poverty. Bardhan claims that there are other factors besides globalization that explain China's increased inequality in recent decades. Bardhan also claims that the large decreases in poverty in China and India may have other explanations, in spite of the fact that the decreases coincide with increased globalization. Bardhan also cautions that concerns about social unrest in China due to inequality are unfounded. Bardhan is professor of economics at the University of California, Berkeley, and author of Awakening Giants, Feet of Clay: Assessing the Economic Rise of China and India.

As you read, consider the following questions:

1. According to Bardhan, what three countries have high inequality?
2. The author cites statistics showing that the majority of the decline in poverty in China occurred prior to what events in the 1990s?
3. Bardhan claims that in China, which is more popular: the central leadership or the local officials?

Economic inequality is on the rise around the world, and many analysts point their fingers at globalization. Are they right?

Globalization and Inequality

Economic inequality has even hit Asia, a region long characterized by relatively low inequality. A report from the Asian Development Bank states that economic inequality now nears the levels of Latin America, a region long characterized by high inequality.

In particular, China, which two decades back was one of the most equal countries in the world, is now among the most unequal countries. Its Gini coefficient—a standard measure of inequality, with zero indicating no inequality and one extreme inequality—for income inequality has now surpassed that of the US. If current trends continue, China may soon reach that of high-inequality countries like Brazil, Mexico and Chile. Bear in mind, such measurements are based on household survey data—therefore most surely underestimate true inequality as there is often large and increasing nonresponse to surveys from richer households.

It is not always clear that globalization is the main force responsible for increased inequality.

The standard reaction in many circles to this phenomenon is that all this must be due to globalization, as Asian countries in general and China in particular have had major global integration during the last two decades. Yes, it is true that when new opportunities open up, the already better-endowed may often be in a better position to utilize them, as well as better equipped to cope with the cold blasts of increased market competition.

But it is not always clear that globalization is the main force responsible for increased inequality. In fact, expansion of labor-intensive industrialization, as has happened in China as the economy opened up, may have helped large numbers of workers. Also, the usual process of economic development involves a major restructuring of the economy, with people moving from agriculture, a sector with low inequality, to other sectors. It is also the case that inequality increased more rapidly in the interior provinces in China than in the more globally exposed coastal provinces. In any case, it is often statistically difficult to disentangle the effects of globalization from those of the ongoing forces of skill-biased technical progress, as with computers; structural and demographic changes; and macroeconomic policies.

Globalization and Poverty

The other reaction, usually on the opposite side, puts aside the issue of inequality and points to the wonders that globalization has done to eliminate extreme poverty, once massive in the two Asian giants, China and India. With global integration of these two economies, it is pointed out that poverty has declined substantially in India and dramatically in China over the last quarter century.

This reaction is also not well founded. While expansion of exports of labor-intensive manufacturing lifted many people out of poverty in China during the last decade (but not in India, where exports are still mainly skill and capital intensive), the more important reason for the dramatic decline of poverty over the last three decades may actually lie elsewhere.

Estimates made at the World Bank suggest that two-thirds of the total decline in the numbers of poor people—below the admittedly crude poverty line of $1 a day per capita—in China between 1981 and 2004 already happened by the mid-1980s, before the big strides in foreign trade and investment in China during the 1990s and later. Much of the extreme poverty was concentrated in rural areas, and its large decline in the first half of the 1980s is perhaps mainly a result of the spurt in agricultural growth following de-collectivization, egalitarian land reform and readjustment of farm procurement prices—mostly internal factors that had little to do with global integration.

The more important reason for the dramatic decline of poverty over the last three decades may actually lie elsewhere.

In India the latest survey data suggest that the rate of decline in poverty somewhat slowed for 1993–2005, the period of intensive opening of the economy, compared to the 1970s and 1980s, and that some child-health indicators, already dismal, have hardly improved in recent years. For example, the percentage of underweight children in India is much larger than in sub-Saharan Africa and has not changed much in the last decade or so. The growth in the agricultural sector, where much of the poverty is concentrated, has declined somewhat in the last decade, largely on account of the decline of public investment in areas like irrigation, which has little to do with globalization.

The Indian pace of poverty reduction has been slower than China's, not just because growth has been much faster in China, but also because the same 1 percent growth rate reduces poverty in India by much less, largely on account of inequalities in wealth—particularly, land and education. Contrary to common perception, these inequalities are much higher in India than in China: The Gini coefficient of land distribution in rural India was 0.74 in 2003; the corresponding figure in China was 0.49 in 2002. India's educational inequality is one of the worst in the world: According to the *World Development Report 2006*, published by the World Bank, the Gini coefficient of the distribution of adult schooling years in the population around 2000 was 0.56 in India, which is not just higher than 0.37 in China, but higher than that of almost all Latin American countries.

Worries About Social Unrest

Another part of the conventional wisdom in the media as well as in academia is how the rising inequality and the inequality-induced grievances, particularly in the left-behind rural areas, cloud the horizon for the future of the Chinese polity and hence economic stability.

Frequently cited evidence of instability comes from Chinese police records, which suggest that incidents of social unrest have multiplied nearly ninefold between 1994 and 2005. While the Chinese leadership is right to be concerned about the inequalities, the conventional wisdom in this matter is somewhat askew, as Harvard sociologist Martin Whyte has pointed out. Data from a 2004 national representative survey in China by his team show that the presumably disadvantaged people in the rural or remote areas are not particularly upset by the rising inequality. This may be because of the familiar "tunnel effect" in the inequality literature: Those who see other people prospering remain hopeful that their chance will come soon, much like drivers in a tunnel, whose hopes rise when blocked traffic in the next lane starts moving. This is particularly so with the relaxation of restrictions on mobility from villages and improvement in roads and transportation.

More than inequality, farmers are incensed by forcible land acquisitions or toxic pollution, but these disturbances are as yet localized. The Chinese leaders have succeeded in deflecting the wrath towards corrupt local officials and in localizing and containing the rural unrest. Opinion surveys suggest that the central leadership is still quite popular, while local officials are not.

Paradoxically, the potential for unrest may be greater in the currently booming urban areas, where the real estate bubble could break. Global recession could ripple through the excess-capacity industries and financially shaky public banks. With more Internet-connected and vocal middle classes, a history of massive worker layoffs and a large underclass of migrants, urban unrest may be more difficult to contain.

Issues like globalization, inequality, poverty and social discontent are thus much more complicated than are allowed in the standard accounts about China and India.

Periodical and Internet Sources Bibliography

The following articles have been selected to supplement the diverse views presented in this chapter.

Jared Bernstein	"Is Education the Cure for Poverty?," *American Prospect*, April 22, 2007.
Gordon Brown	"To Combat Poverty, Get Africa's Children to School," *Financial Times*, September 19, 2010.
William Easterly	"Measuring How and Why Aid Works—or Doesn't," *Wall Street Journal*, April 30, 2011.
Katrin Elborgh-Woytek and Robert Gregory	"Poorest Economies Can Export More," *Finance & Development*, December 2010.
Glenn Hubbard	"Only Local Business Can End Global Poverty," *Financial Times*, July 23, 2009.
Mark Lange	"A First Step for the Global Poor—Shatter Six Myths," *Christian Science Monitor*, March 10, 2008.
Dambisa Moyo	"Capitalism for Africa," *Guardian* (UK), February 26, 2009.
Baldev Raj Nayar	"India: Poverty Retreats with Globalization's Advance," *YaleGlobal Online*, February 1, 2007. http://yaleglobal.yale.edu.
Martin Ravallion and Dominique van de Walle	"Land and Poverty in Reforming East Asia," *Finance & Development*, September 2008.
Simon Rosenblum and Lorraine Copas	"The Choice: Lower Child Poverty or Lower Corporate Taxes," *Vancouver Sun*, April 29, 2011.
Erin Wildermuth	"Money Won't Cure Global Poverty," *American Spectator*, July 10, 2008.

For Further Discussion

Chapter 1

1. The United Nations notes that the global financial crisis slowed progress in fighting poverty but is cautiously optimistic about the poverty rate falling below 15 percent by 2015. Name one specific way that Laurence Chandy and Geoffrey Gertz disagree with the United Nations.

2. David Woodward criticizes the method for assessing poverty that uses a dollar amount rather than assessing rights. Which of the other authors in this chapter utilize the method Woodward criticizes?

Chapter 2

1. Based on the viewpoint of Ejaz Ghani and the viewpoint of Farrukh Iqbal and Mustapha Kamel Nabli, in what way is poverty similar in South Asia and in the Middle East and North Africa?

2. What is the primary difference between the way poverty is measured in Africa by Maxim Pinkovskiy and Xavier Sala-i-Martin, and the way poverty is calculated in high-income countries by Timothy Smeeding?

Chapter 3

1. What is a counterexample that Nicholas Eberstadt gives to the argument—made by the United Nations Population Fund—that population growth leads to poverty?

2. Explain how the World Food Programme might respond to Abhijit Banerjee and Esther Duflo's skepticism about the hunger-poverty trap.

Chapter 4

1. Kevin Watkins disputes Dambisa Moyo's proposal for ending foreign aid to Africa. Despite this disagreement, name at least one point on which they both agree.

2. Claire Melamed and Arvind Panagariya both stress the importance of redistribution to alleviate poverty. How do their proposed redistribution schemes differ?

Organizations to Contact

The editors have compiled the following list of organizations concerned with the issues debated in this book. The descriptions are derived from materials provided by the organizations. All have publications or information available for interested readers. The list was compiled on the date of publication of the present volume; the information provided here may change. Be aware that many organizations take several weeks or longer to respond to inquiries, so allow as much time as possible.

American Enterprise Institute for Public Policy Research (AEI)

1150 Seventeenth Street NW, Washington, DC   20036
(202) 862-5800 • fax: (202) 862-7177
e-mail: webmaster@aei.org
website: www.aei.org

The American Enterprise Institute for Public Policy Research (AEI) is a private, nonpartisan, not-for-profit organization dedicated to research and education on issues of government, politics, economics, and social welfare. AEI sponsors research and publishes materials toward the end of defending the principles, and improving the institutions, of American freedom and democratic capitalism. Among AEI's publications is the book *Prices, Poverty, and Inequality: Why Americans Are Better Off than You Think.*

Center for American Progress (CAP)

1333 H Street NW, 10th Floor, Washington, DC   20005
(202) 682-1611 • fax: (202) 682-1867
website: www.americanprogress.org

The Center for American Progress (CAP) is a nonprofit, nonpartisan organization dedicated to improving the lives of Americans through progressive ideas and action. CAP dialogues with leaders, thinkers, and citizens to explore the vital issues facing America and the world. CAP publishes numerous research papers, which are available at its website, including "Top 10 Striking Findings from the Latest Data on Poverty: Millions of Americans Continue to Wrestle with Economic Hardship."

Centre for Economic Policy Research (CEPR)

77 Bastwick Street, London   EC1V 3PZ
    United Kingdom
(44) 20 7183 8801 • fax: (44) 20 7183 8820
e-mail: cepr@cepr.org
website: www.cepr.org

The Centre for Economic Policy Research (CEPR) is the leading European research network in economics. CEPR conducts research through a network of academic outlets and disseminates the results to the private sector and policy community. CEPR produces a wide range of reports, books, and conference volumes each year, including the book *Food Prices and Rural Poverty*.

Children's Defense Fund (CDF)

25 E Street NW, Washington, DC   20001
(800) 233-1200
e-mail: cdfinfo@childrensdefense.org
website: www.childrensdefense.org

The Children's Defense Fund (CDF) is a nonprofit child advocacy organization that works to ensure a level playing field for all American children, particularly poor and minority children and those with disabilities. The organization champions policies and programs that lift children out of poverty, including the Head Start and Healthy Start programs. The CDF publishes many reports, including "The Impact of Rising Poverty on the Nation's Young Families and Their Children, 2000–2010."

Economic Policy Institute (EPI)

1333 H Street NW, Suite 300, East Tower
Washington, DC   20005-4707
(202) 775-8810 • fax: (202) 775-0819
e-mail: epi@epi.org
website: www.epi.org

The Economic Policy Institute (EPI) is a nonprofit Washington, DC, think tank that seeks to broaden the discussion about economic policy to include the interests of low- and middle-income workers. EPI briefs policy makers at all levels of government; provides technical support to national, state, and local activists and community organizations; testifies before national, state, and local legislatures; and provides information and background to the print and electronic media. EPI publishes books, studies, issue briefs, popular education materials, and other publications, among which is the biennially published *State of Working America.*

Global Policy Forum (GPF) Europe

Koenigstrasse 37a, Bonn   D-53115
   Germany
(49) 228 965 0510 • fax: (49) 228 963 8206
e-mail: europe@globalpolicy.org
website: www.globalpolicy.org/gpf-europe

Global Policy Forum (GPF) Europe is a nonprofit organization with consultative status at the United Nations (UN). The mission of GPF Europe is to monitor European policy making at the UN, promote accountability of global decisions, educate and mobilize for global citizen participation, and advocate on vital issues of international peace and justice. GPF Europe publishes policy papers, articles, and statements, including the briefing paper "Thinking Ahead: Development Models and Indicators of Well-Being Beyond the MDGs."

International Monetary Fund (IMF)

700 Nineteenth Street NW, Washington, DC   20431
(202) 623-7000 • fax: (202) 623-4661

e-mail: publicaffairs@imf.org
website: www.imf.org

The International Monetary Fund (IMF) is an organization of 186 countries that work to foster global monetary cooperation, secure financial stability, facilitate international trade, promote high employment and sustainable economic growth, and reduce poverty around the world. The IMF monitors the world's economies, lends to members in economic difficulty, and provides technical assistance. The IMF publishes fact sheets, reports on key issues, and the *IMF Annual Report.*

Oxfam International
Suite 20, 266 Banbury Road, Oxford   OX2 7DL
   United Kingdom
(44) 1865 339 100 • fax: (44) 1865 339 101
e-mail: enquiries@oxfam.org.uk
website: www.oxfam.org

Oxfam International is a confederation of organizations working to end poverty and injustice. Oxfam works to create programs to eradicate poverty and combat injustice, delivers life-saving assistance to people affected by natural disasters or conflict, and aims to raise public awareness of the causes of poverty. Oxfam publishes research and analysis, available at its website, such as "Living on a Spike: How Is the 2011 Food Price Crisis Affecting Poor People?"

United Nations (UN)
760 United Nations Plaza, New York, NY   10017
(212) 906-5000 • fax: (212) 906-5001
website: www.un.org

The United Nations (UN) is an international organization of 193 member states committed to maintaining international peace and security; developing friendly relations among nations; and promoting social progress, better living standards, and human rights. The United Nations spearheaded the development of the Millennium Development Goals, aimed at encouraging development by improving social and economic conditions in the world's poorest countries. The UN publishes numerous annual human development reports and publications on the achievement of the Millennium Development Goals.

World Bank

1818 H Street NW, Washington, DC   20433
(202) 473-1000 • fax: (202) 477-6391
website: www.worldbank.org

The World Bank is made up of two unique development institutions owned by 187 member countries: the International Bank for Reconstruction and Development (IBRD) and the International Development Association (IDA). The World Bank provides low-interest loans, interest-free credits, and grants to developing countries for a wide array of purposes. It publishes the annual *World Development Report* and *World Development Indicators*.

Bibliography of Books

Abhijit V. Banerjee and Esther Duflo — *Poor Economics: A Radical Rethinking of the Way to Fight Global Poverty.* New York: PublicAffairs, 2011.

Lael Brainard, Abigail Jones, and Nigel Purvis, eds. — *Climate Change and Global Poverty: A Billion Lives in the Balance?* Washington, DC: Brookings Institution Press, 2009.

Glynn Cochrane — *Festival Elephants and the Myth of Global Poverty.* Boston, MA: Pearson, 2009.

Paul Collier — *The Bottom Billion: Why the Poorest Countries Are Failing and What Can Be Done About It.* New York: Oxford University Press, 2007.

Nicholas Eberstadt — *The Poverty of "The Poverty Rate": Measure and Mismeasure of Want in Modern America.* Washington, DC: AEI Press, 2008.

Abigail Gosselin — *Global Poverty and Individual Responsibility.* Lanham, MD: Lexington Books, 2009.

Duncan Green — *From Poverty to Power: How Active Citizens and Effective States Can Change the World.* Oxford, England: Oxfam International, 2008.

Peter Greer and Phil Smith — *The Poor Will Be Glad: Joining the Revolution to Lift the World Out of Poverty.* Grand Rapids, MI: Zondervan, 2009.

David Hulme   *Global Poverty: How Global Gover-
                           nance Is Failing the Poor.* New York:
                           Routledge, 2010.

Charles Karelis   *The Persistence of Poverty: Why the
                           Economics of the Well-Off Can't Help
                           the Poor.* New Haven, CT: Yale Uni-
                           versity Press, 2007.

Dean Karlan and   *More than Good Intentions: How a
Jacob Appel   New Economics Is Helping to Solve
                           Global Poverty.* New York: Dutton,
                           2011.

Stephen Pimpare   *A People's History of Poverty in
                           America.* New York: New Press, 2008.

Paul Polak   *Out of Poverty: What Works When
                           Traditional Approaches Fail.* San Fran-
                           cisco, CA: Berrett-Koehler, 2008.

Ananya Roy   *Poverty Capital: Microfinance and the
                           Making of Development.* New York:
                           Routledge, 2010.

Phil Smith and   *A Billion Bootstraps: Microcredit,
Eric Thurman   Barefoot Banking, and the Business
                           Solution for Ending Poverty.* New
                           York: McGraw-Hill, 2007.

Stephen C. Smith   *Ending Global Poverty: A Guide to
                           What Works.* New York: Palgrave
                           Macmillan, 2005.

William T.   *Poor People.* New York: Ecco, 2007.
Vollmann

Jeffrey G.
Williamson

Trade and Poverty: When the Third World Fell Behind. Cambridge, MA: MIT Press, 2011.

Quentin Wodon,
ed.

Migration, Remittances, and Poverty: Case Studies from West Africa. Washington, DC: World Bank, 2006.

Muhammad
Yunus with Karl
Weber

Creating a World Without Poverty: Social Business and the Future of Capitalism. New York: PublicAffairs, 2007.

Index

Geographic headings and page numbers in **boldface** refer to viewpoints about that country or region.